CW00740784

# STANIER BLACK FIVE LOCOMOTIVES

# STANIER BLACK FIVE LOCOMOTIVES

Keith Langston

PEN & SWORD
TRANSPORT

First published in Great Britain in 2018 by
Pen & Sword Transport
An imprint of Pen & Sword Books Ltd
47 Church Street
Barnsley
South Yorkshire
S70 2AS

Copyright © Keith Langston, 2018

ISBN 978 1 52671 905 8

The right of Keith Langston to be identified as the author of this work
has been asserted by him in accordance with the Copyright, Designs
and Patents Act 1988. All rights reserved. No part of this publication
may be reproduced or transmitted in any form or by any means,
electronic or mechanical, including photocopy, recording or any
information storage and retrieval system, without the prior written
permission of the publisher, nor by way of trade or otherwise shall it be
lent, re-sold, hired out or otherwise circulated without the publisher's
prior consent in any form of binding or cover other than that in which
it is published and without a similar condition including this condition
being imposed on the subsequent purchaser.

Typeset in Palatino by Mac Style
Printed and bound by Replika Press Pvt Ltd.

Pen & Sword Books Ltd incorporates the imprints of Pen & Sword
Archaeology, Atlas, Aviation, Battleground, Discovery, Family History,
History, Maritime, Military, Naval, Politics, Railways, Select, Social
History, Transport, True Crime, and Claymore Press, Frontline Books,
Leo Cooper, Praetorian Press, Remember When, Seaforth Publishing
and Wharncliffe.

For a complete list of Pen and Sword titles please contact:
Pen and Sword Books Limited
47 Church Street, Barnsley, South Yorkshire, S70 2AS, England
E-mail: enquiries@pen-and-sword.co.uk
Website: www.pen-and-sword.co.uk

# CONTENTS

## Sir William Arthur Stanier
### (27 May 1876–27 September 1965)

Educated Wycliffe College.
Trained G.W.R. Swindon. Apprentice 1892–97.

Senior Positions:
1904, Ass. to Divisional Loco. Supt., London.
1906, Ass. to Swindon Works Manager.
1912, Ass. Works Manager, Swindon.
1920, Swindon Works Manager.
1922, Principal Ass. to C.M.E.
1932–44, C.M.E. of L.M.S.
1942, Scientific Adviser to Min. of Production.
1943, Director of Power-Jets Ltd.

Honours:
1936 and 1938, President, I.L.E.
1941, President, I.M.E.
1943, Knighted.
1944, Fellow of Royal Society.
1945, Honorary Member of I.M.E.
1957, I.L.E. Gold Medal.
1963, I.M.E. James Watt International Medal.

C.M.E Chief Mechanical Engineer.
I.L.E. Institution of Locomotive Engineers.
I.M.E Institution of Mechanical Engineers.

## 5MT 44658-45499
### 4-6-0 LMS Stanier 'Black Five'

Power Classification 5MT (Mixed Traffic)
Introduced 1934–1951 LMS/BR

| | |
|---|---|
| Weight: | Loco 72t 2cwt |
| | Caprotti Loco 74t 0cwt |
| | (Skefko, Timken, Stephenson valve gear) Loco 75t 6cwt |
| Tender: | (Coal capacity 9 tons, water 4000gals) 54t 13cwt |
| Tender Wheel: | 4ft 3in dia |
| Driving Wheel: | 6ft 0in dia |
| Bogie Wheel: | 3ft 3½in dia |
| Boiler Pressure: | (Superheated) 225 psi |
| Cylinders: | (outside) 18½ in x 28 in |
| Tractive Effort: | (at 85% boiler pressure) 25455lbf |
| Valve Gear: | Walschaert (piston valves) |
| | Inside Caprotti (poppet valves) |
| | Outside Caprotti (poppet valves) |
| | Outside Stephenson (piston valves) |
| Length over buffers: | (Wheelbase 53ft 2¾in) 63ft 7¾in |
| Timken/Walschaert Ivatt: | (Wheelbase 53ft 6¾in) 63ft 11¾in |
| Timken/Caprotti Ivatt: | (Wheelbase 53ft 6¾in) 63ft 11¾in |

842 locomotives built: Crewe Works 241, Derby Works 54
Horwich 120 and by contractors Armstrong Whitworth, Newcastle-on-Tyne 327,
Vulcan Foundry, Newton le Willows 100.

# CHAPTER 1

# INTRODUCTION: LMS 'BLACK FIVE'

The Stanier 5MT (Class 5) 4-6-0 became colloquially known as the 'Black Five', from a combination of the LMS colour and power classification. However, in the early years the 2-cylinder locomotive design was often referred to by the name 'Black Stanier' in order to distinguish it from the designers then LMS red liveried 3-cylinder 'Jubilee' class. Even to the unpractised eye Stanier's 5MT design bore similarities in appearance to the more powerful 'Jubilee' engines. Similarly, in outward appearance the Belpaire firebox and sloping boiler combination of either class could well have indicated that they were Great Western Railway (GWR) Swindon Works products! However, Stanier followed LMS practice by adding outside Walschaerts valve gear.

## William A. Stanier

Stanier was famously 'headhunted' in late 1931 by the London Midland & Scottish Railway (LMS) when that organisation's chairman Sir Josiah Stamp recognised his burgeoning talents. Early promotion chances for Stanier were limited at the GWR and therefore he was reportedly happy to switch from Swindon to Crewe, doing so in January 1932. Employing the benefit of hindsight, it is easy to see that the GWR's loss was very much the LMS's gain. It is said that Stanier brought with him a chest containing a large number of working drawings, but undoubtedly his greatest asset was 40 years of locomotive design and operational experience.

Stanier designed/converted 14 LMS steam locomotive classes (comprising 2431 engines) of which the 'Black Fives' with a build total of 842 were his fifth project.

The first of the class appeared in August 1934 having been built by the contractors Vulcan Foundry, and not as should have been the case by Crewe Works! No doubt there were some red faces at Crewe who failed to turn out their first of the class, LMS No 5000 until the following year.

An interesting aside is that Stanier wrote to Edward Thompson of the London North Eastern Railway (LNER) on 16 January 1943 in order to congratulate him on the design of his 'B1' class 2-cylinder 4-6-0s, in which he saw similarities with the 'Black Five'. Thompsons reply is worthy of note:

> 19 Jan'43,
> My dear Stanier,
> Thank you very much for your letter of the 16th. After all, what is my new one but a 'Black Stanier' to LNER standards
> Yours ever
> (signed) Edward Thompson

### Requirement

As early as 1924 Mr J.H. Follows, the then LMSR Operating Superintendent had asked the board for an engine that would 'go anywhere and do anything'. Some ten years later Stanier answered that call with his 'Black Five' design which the LMSR then termed a 'universal' locomotive. So great was the LMSR need for a new 'Class 5' that the first orders were placed straight off the drawing board with Crewe Works and Vulcan Foundry receiving the first orders during 1933–4 (LMS lot Nos 114 and 119).

The specification adhered to was that the new 2-cylinder 4-6-0 tender engine could work over at least 70 per cent of the company's routes, whilst being rostered to haul approximately the same amount of freight and passenger trains.

Stanier's early boilers were constructed domeless (regulator housed in the smokebox) and with low-degree 14 element superheaters. In service they were less than satisfactory. To overcome the drawbacks Stanier quickly revised the design to incorporate larger (28 element) superheaters. He also replaced the troublesome smokebox regulator with the more reliable dome type.

All the boilers for the 415 railway-built locomotives were manufactured at Crewe Works, irrespective of which works was responsible for constructing the engines. However, the private makers (contractors) built the boilers for the 427 locomotives which they supplied.

The private builders, Vulcan Foundry (VF) and Armstrong Whitworth (AW) were responsible for 50.5 per cent of the total build. The second order placed with AW, for some 227 locomotives and tenders was the largest single locomotive contract ever placed by a British railway company. Completion of that order, with promised short delivery dates, was made possible by a government loan made under the Railways (Agreement) Act of 20 December 1935.

### Cost Comparisons
### (LMS Sanctioned costs)

Armstrong Whitworth locomotives authorised in November 1934 (built 1935) covered by LMS Lot No 124 showed a sanctioned cost of £5,119 for locomotive and tender. Running Nos LMS 5125–5224.

That figure can be compared with the first 20 Crewe built locomotives authorised in April 1934 (1935) and covered by Lot No 114 which showed a higher sanctioned cost of £6,500 per locomotive and tender. Running Nos LMS 5000–5019.

The first of the Vulcan Foundry built locomotives (1935) which were authorised in June 1934 and covered by LMS Lot No 123, running Nos 5075–5124 and the second batch of Crewe locomotives authorised in June 1934 (built 1935) and covered by LMS Lot No 122, running

Stanier 'Black Five'
BR No 44868 at Heaton
Mersey. *Keith Langston
Collection*

Nos LMS 5070–5074 both showed a cost of £6,150 per locomotive and tender.

However, the aforementioned Armstrong Whitworth order for 227 locomotives authorised in January 1936 (built 1936–7) and covered by LMS Lot No 131 showed a sanctioned cost of £6,080 per locomotive and tender. Running Nos LMS 5225–5451.

Costs for orders completed by all of the manufacturing centres continued at an average cost of £6,455 per locomotive and tender for all those authorised up to and including January 1938 (LMS Lots 142 (built 1938) LMS running Nos 5452–5471, 151 and 152 LMS running Nos 5472–5496 and 153 LMS running Nos 5497–5499 and 4800–4806 (built 1943–4).

Orders authorised during 1943 under LMS Lot Nos 170 (1943–4) and 174 (1945–6) for locomotives built at Derby, Crewe and Horwich Works showed a cost of £9,500 per locomotive and tender. LMS running Nos 4807–4966.

That cost rose to £9,575 for Lot No 183 (1946–7) locomotive and tenders built at Crewe and Horwich Works. LMS running Nos 4967–4996.

Orders authorised during 1945 built at Horwich Works (1947–8) under LMS Lot No 187 showed a cost of £10,538 per locomotive and tender. Running Nos LMS 4997–4999, 4783–4789 and 4790–4799.

Orders authorised during 1945 built at Crewe Works (1947–8) under LMS Lot No 187 showed a cost of £10,538 per locomotive and tender. Running Nos LMS 4768–4782, 4758–4767, 4748–4757 and BR 44738–44747.

Orders authorised during 1946 built at Horwich Works (1948–49) under BR Lot No 192 showed a cost of £10,125 per locomotive and tender. Running Nos BR 44698–44717.

Orders authorised during 1946 built at Crewe Works (1948–49) under BR Lot No 192 showed a cost of £10,125 per locomotive and tender. Running Nos BR 44718–44737.

Orders authorised during 1947 built at Crewe Works under Lot No 199 showed a cost of £14,175 per locomotive and tender. Running Nos BR 44658–44667. Orders authorised during 1947 built at Horwich Works under Lot No 199 showed a cost of £14,175 per locomotive and tender. Running Nos BR 44668–44697.

The costs shown are the official sanctioned amounts at the time of order. However, from 1944 onwards the 'sanctioned costs' of some locomotives show some significant interesting variations from the recorded 'actual costs'.

Caprotti 'Black Five'
BR No 44687.
*Keith Langston Collection*

| Locomotives | Sanctioned £ | Actual £ |
|---|---|---|
| 4748-4754 | 10,538 | 14,941 |
| 4755-4757 | 10,538 | 15,325 |
| 4758-4764 | 10,538 | 13,127 |
| 4765-4766 | 10,538 | 13,440 |
| 4767 | 10,538 | 13,728 |
| 4768-4782 | 10,538 | 10,646 |
| 4683-4799 | 10,538 | 13,423 |
| 4982-4996 | 10,538 | 12,903 |
| 4997-4999 | 10,538 | 13,413 |
| 44658 | 14,175 | 12,280 |
| 44659-44667 | 14,175 | 12,101 |
| 44668-44677 | 14,175 | 14,748 |
| 44678-44685 | 14,175 | 16,235 |
| 44686-44687 | 14,175 | 20,642 |
| 44688-44695 | 14,175 | 15,018 |
| 44696-44697 | 14,175 | 16,424 |
| 44698-44717 | 10,125 | 14,450 |
| 44718-44727 | 10,125 | 11,580 |
| 44728-44737 | 10,125 | 11,826 |
| 44738-44747 | 10,538 | 13,470 |

## LMSR 'Black Five' build details:

| Intro | Build total | Lot No | Works | Running Numbers |
|---|---|---|---|---|
| 1935 | 20 | 114 | Crw | 5000-19 |
| 1934-5 | 50 | 119 | VF | 5020-69 |
| 1935 | 5 | 122 | Crw | 5070-74 |
| 1935 | 50 | 123 | VF | 5075-5124 |
| 1935 | 100 | 124 | AW | 5125-5224 |
| 1936-7 | 227 | 131 | AW | 5225-5451 |
| 1938 | 20 | 142 | Crw | 5452-5471 |
| 1943-4 | 10 | 151 | Der | 5472-5481 |

| Intro | Build total | Lot No | Works | Running Numbers |
|---|---|---|---|---|
| 1943-4 | 15 | 152 | Der | 5482-5496 |
| 1943-4 | 10 | 153 | Der | 5497-5499 4800-4806 |
| 1943-4 | 19 | 170 | Der | 4807-4825 |
| 1943-4 | 10 | 170 | Crw | 4826-4835 |
| 1943-4 | 10 | 170 | Crw | 4836-4845 |
| 1943-4 | 10 | 170 | Crw | 4846-4855 |
| 1943-4 | 10 | 170 | Crw | 4856-4865 |
| 1943-4 | 6 | 170 | Crw | 4866-4871 |
| 1945-6 | 20 | 174 | Crw | 4872-4891 |
| 1945-6 | 20 | 174 | Crw | 4892-4911 |
| 1945-6 | 20 | 174 | Crw | 4912-4931 |
| 1945-6 | 10 | 174 | Hor | 4932-4941 |
| 1945-6 | 25 | 174 | Hor | 4942-4966 |

| Intro | Build total | Lot No | Works | Running Numbers |
|---|---|---|---|---|
| 1946-7 | 15 | 183 | Crw | 4967-4981 |
| 1946-7 | 15 | 183 | Hor | 4982-4996 |
| 1947-8 | 10 | 187 | Hor | 4997-4999 4783-4789 |
| 1947-8 | 10 | 187 | Hor | 4790-4799 |
| 1947-8 | 15 | 187 | Crw | 4768-4782 |
| 1947-8 | 10 | 187 | Crw | 4758-4767 |
| 1947-8 | 10 | 187 | Crw | 4748-4757 |
| 1947-8 | 10 | 187 | Crw | 44738-44747 |
| 1948-9 | 20 | 192 | Hor | 44698-44717 |
| 1948-9 | 20 | 192 | Crw | 44718-44737 |
| 1949-51 | 10 | 199 | Crw | 44658-44667 |
| 1949-51 | 30 | 199 | Hor | 44668-44697 |

*AW-Armstrong Whitworth, Crw-Crewe. Der-Derby Hor-Horwich, VF-Vulcan Foundry*

## The locomotives

With their weight and length statistics the Stanier 'Black Five' locomotives had, as intended, virtually total access to the entire LMSR system. The versatile engines were able to handle 'loose' and 'fitted' goods trains (i.e. fully vacuum-braked) and importantly semi-fast and also express passenger services.

The design's free steaming abilities in conjunction with Stanier's precise valve settings allowed speeds in the region of 90mph to be achieved. Initial running tests with 50 per cent of the reciprocating weights being balanced proved to be satisfactory.

The locomotives were placed in power class 5 by the LMS and throughout their working lives this was displayed on the cabside sheets in several ways, i.e. 5MT, 5P5F and simply 5.

The original length over buffers of the class was 63ft 7¾ in (coupled wheelbase 27ft 2in) with 7ft + 8ft coupled wheel spacing. Total wheelbase engine and tender 53ft 2¾in.

The length over buffers of the later built locomotives including (Ivatt types) was longer at 63ft 11¾in (coupled wheelbase 27ft 6in) with 7ft + 8ft 4in coupled wheel spacing. Total wheelbase engine and tender 53ft 6¾in.

Stanier 'Black Five' 45101 is seen at Manchester Exchange station. *Keith Langston Collection*

Motion and bearing details:

| BR Nos | Valve motion | Bearings | Wheel base ft in |
|---|---|---|---|
| 44658–67 | Walschaerts | Plain | 27 – 6 |
| 44668–77 | Walschaerts | SKF driving axle | 27 – 6 |
| 44678–85 | Walschaerts | SKF all axles | 27 – 6 |
| 44686–87 | Caprotti outside | SKF all axles | 27 – 6 |
| 44688–97 | Walschaerts | Timken driving axle | 27 – 6 |
| 44698–737 | Walschaerts | Plain | 27 – 6 |
| 44738–47 | Caprotti inside | Plain | 27 – 6 |
| 44748–57 | Caprotti inside | Timken all axles | 27 – 6 |
| 44758–66 | Walschaerts | Timken all axles | 27 – 6 |
| 44767 | Stephenson | Timken all axles | 27 – 6 |
| 44768–45499 | Walschaerts | Plain | 27 – 2 |

Because of wartime restrictions the 'Black Five' build programme was halted after 1938 and it recommenced in April 1943 just one year before the retirement of Stanier from the LMSR.

In the opinion of many observers Stanier's 'Black Five' was the most efficient design of mixed traffic locomotive ever to be introduced in Great Britain. In keeping with the LMSR's intentions, the type did prove to be a true 'maid of all work' and with almost universal route availability they could be seen on the LMSR network from Thurso in the far north of Scotland to Bournemouth in the south of England. Later under BR on what would have been previously considered 'enemy territory'! A fact borne out by the many and diverse locations shown in this publication's chosen images.

Indeed, the locations themselves are very much a part of railway history in general and the 'Black Five' story in particular.

## Boilers

In addition to Stanier's initial boiler alterations there were other modifications. Some of which changed the external appearance of the locomotives. One major change not easily discernible was the switch from vertical throatplate to sloping throatplate boilers.

Locomotives LMS Nos 5000–5006 and 5020 to 5069 were built with the original vertical throatplate LMS '3B' type domeless boiler with 14-element superheaters.

Locomotives LMS Nos 5070–5224 and 5007–5019 retained the same boiler pattern but with 21-element superheaters. All of those boilers were interchangeable.

Sloping throatplate domed boilers were introduced with the 1936 batch of 227 locomotives built by Armstrong Whitworth, LMS Nos 5225–5451. Simply put, the throatplate was inclined forward approximately 10½in from the foundation ring which resulted in a 12in shorter barrel and tube length. The 1935–37 built engines had larger grates and a proportionately greater heating surface, also they were fitted with 24-element superheaters. The boilers were fitted with a top feed located on the second ring of the boiler barrel and the regulator was situated in the dome.

The engines built after 1938 were given 28-element superheaters and the top feed was located on the first ring of the boiler barrel. The external appearance of any particular 'Black Five' can be misleading when trying to confirm build date etc, as much changing of boilers took place during the working lives of the engines.

Several combinations of the number and sizes of boiler tubes and flues were used throughout the working life of the class.

Preserved outside Stephenson valve gear 'Black Five' BR No 44767 GEORGE STEPHENSON is seen at Mallaig in June 1986. *John Chalcraft/Rail Photoprints*

## Names

Although names have been given to preserved members of the class, in reality only 4 members of the class ever carried a name during their LMS/BR service. They were:

BR No 45154 LANARKSHIRE YEOMANRY      BR No 45156 AYRSHIRE YEOMANRY
BR No 45157 THE GLASGOW HIGHLANDER      BR No 45158 GLASGOW YEOMANRY

Reportedly one locomotive carried a name between 1942 and 1944: BR No 45155 THE QUEEN'S EDINBURGH, but conclusive evidence of nameplates being cast has never been found.

The Riddles designed (1951–57) BR Standard 'Class 5' 4-6-0 design could rightly be described as a further development of the Stanier 'Black Five'.

After the retirement of Stanier, Charles Fairburn became CME of the LMSR but during his short tenure no significant changes were made to the 'Black Five' design. However, the same cannot be said of the next man to occupy that post, one Henry George Ivatt who took over on 1 February 1946. After the creation of British Railways BR (1948) Ivatt reverted to the role of CME London Midland Region until his retirement in 1951, and Robert Riddles became the CME of BR.

## Experimental modifications

Locomotives BR Nos 44738 – 44757 fitted with inside *Caprotti valve gear and low running plates.*
Locomotives BR Nos 44686 and 44687 fitted *with outside Caprotti valve gear and high running plates.*
Locomotives BR Nos 44686 and 44687, 44755 – 44757 (1948), 44765–44767 *fitted with double chimneys.*
Locomotives BR Nos 44718–44727 *fitted with steel fireboxes.*
Locomotives BR Nos 44826 and 44827, 44829 and 44830 and 44844 were *converted to oil-burning in 1947 and converted back to coal in 1948.*
Locomotives BR Nos 44678–44687 *fitted with Skefko roller bearings throughout.*
Locomotives BR Nos 44668–44677 *fitted with Skefko roller bearing on driving coupled axle.*
Locomotives BR No 44767 *fitted with outside Stephenson valve gear.*
Locomotives BR No 44748–44767 *fitted with Timken roller bearings throughout.*
Locomotive BR Nos 44688–44697 *fitted with Timken roller bearings on driving coupled axles.*

## Maximum axle load

Route availability is directly related to axle load. In that regard the 'Black Five' locomotives compared well with other LMS/BR 4-6-0 locomotives of the era. Having an average axle loading of 18.2 tons, from a minimum of 17.8 tons, and after taking into account the design variants to a maximum of 19.45 tons.

In comparison Stanier's 'Jubilee' class had an approximate average axle loading of 20 tons. The original 'Royal Scot' class locomotives had a maximum axle loading of 20.9 tons, whilst in re-built form that figure was reduced slightly to 20.5 tons.

## Tenders

In all instances the capacity of 'Black Five' tenders remained the same i.e. 9 tons of coal and 4000 gallons of water. However, there were variations in construction method. When new, the early batches of locomotives were all coupled to tenders of rivetted construction. Those were later superseded by all welded construction tenders. The Ivatt type locomotives were originally coupled with combined rivetted and welded construction tenders. Tare weight varied during the construction period from 26.8 tons to 27.9 tons. The weight variations being determined by construction type with the fully welded type being the lightest. All of the tender types were fitted with a handscrew-operated water pick up equipment (scoop). Vacuum controlled tender steam brakes were also fitted, and those operated with the locomotives equipment.

All tenders were of a 3-axle design with outside axle boxes and 4ft 3in diameter wheels. The LMSR constructed four self-weighing tenders which were in regular use. During the working life of locomotives, a degree of tender swopping took place.

## Other notable modifications

A majority of the 'Black Fives' operating on the Scottish network were fitted with tablet catchers to facilitate working over single line sections. In addition, small buffer beam type snowploughs were also fitted.

From 1958 onwards, Automatic Warning System (AWS) was gradually installed. Locomotives thus fitted had a protection plate added behind the buffer beam front coupling, with the associated small cylindrical reservoir on the running plate and in front of the cab.

Electric lighting for headlights and driving cab was installed in 1947–48 on locomotives BR Nos 44658, 44755–57 and LMS Nos 4765–67. The Stone's turbo generating sets and lighting were removed during 1952–53 because of defects encountered during normal running.

Boilers with self-cleaning smoke boxes were first introduced during 1945. All of the locomotives so fitted carried a cast plate 'SC' on the lower part of the smoke box door usually below the shed code plate. The illustrated section of this publication details locomotives in year and month of build (to service) order. The Appendix however lists the 'Black Fives' in the BR number series.

Not all the 842 locomotives are illustrated but representative examples of each year, boiler type and variation(s) have been included.

Combined cast shed plate and self-cleaning plate, circa 1950.

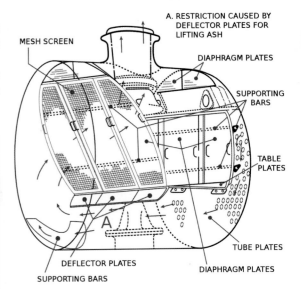

Self-cleaning smokebox diagram.

Preserved Stanier 'Black Five' BR No 45337 is seen on shed at the Llangollen Railway (LR) in August 2014.
*Fred Kerr*

## Stanier 'Black Five' 4-6-0 Locomotives. Total built 842 LMS/BR 1934/51 – 18 examples preserved.

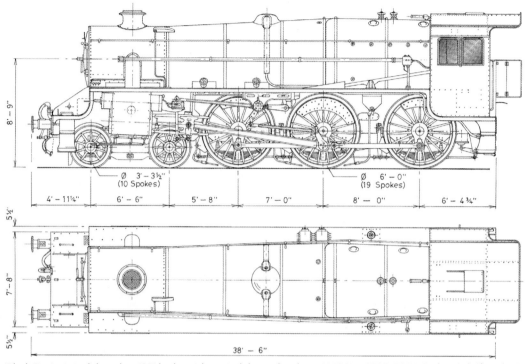

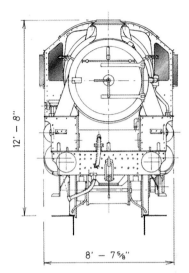

Front end view. Train heating hose below buffer beam.

'Black Five' original domeless '3B' boiler with vertical throatplate locos LMS Nos 5000–5224. Boiler pitch (ft and in) 8–9. Belpaire firebox with a grate area of 27.8sqft, 2 x 2½in pop safety valves. Walschaerts-motion, coupled wheelbase 7ft+8ft, total wheelbase 53ft 2¾in. Loco and tender length over buffers 63ft 7¾in. Tapered rectangular section coupling rods, I section driving rods.

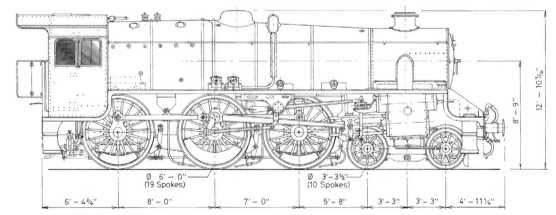

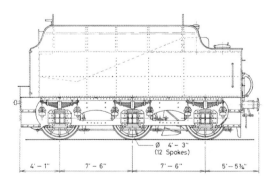

Locomotive with sloping throat plate (from loco LMS No 5225 onwards, '3B' domed boiler with top feed on 2nd (centre) ring of boiler barrel, feed pipe over boiler cladding. Boiler pitch (ft and in) 8–9. Belpaire firebox with a grate area of 28.65sqft. Two mechanical lubricators located on right-hand running plate, one of 12 feeds for cylinders, valves and glands and one of 8 feeds for the coupled axles, both driven from the top of the right-hand combination lever. Sandbox 3ft long filler necks brought up above running plate level. Tapered rectangular section coupling rods, I section driving rods.

Coal 9 ton, watewr 9000 gallon.

*All drawings by Ian Beattie, courtesy of* Railway Modeller *magazine.* www.pecopublications.co.uk

Outside Caprotti valve motion. Double blastpipe and chimney. Domed '3B' boiler with top feed mounted on front ring of boiler barrel, feed pipe under cladding. Boiler pitch (ft and in) 8-11. High running plate and extended length sandbox filler necks. There were two mechanical lubricators located on right-hand running plate which was constructed in two sections to suit. Coupled wheelbase 7ft+8ft 4in, total wheelbase 53ft 6¾in. Loco and tender length over buffers 63ft 11¾in. I section coupling and driving rods. Open-work footsteps.

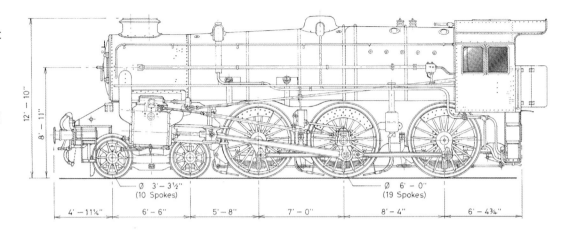

Inside Timken Caprotti valve motion. Low running plate set level with the top of the Caprotti box, three separate splashers per side. Domed '3B' boiler with top feed mounted on front ring of boiler barrel, feed pipe under cladding. There were two mechanical lubricators located on right-hand running plate. Coupled wheelbase 7ft+8ft 4in, total wheelbase 53ft 6¾in. Loco and tender length over buffers 63ft 11¾in. I section coupling and driving rods. Open-work footsteps.

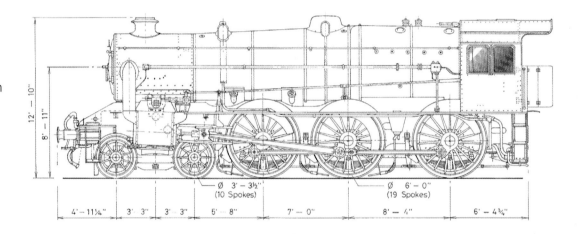

Walschaerts valve gear with outside Stephenson motion incorporating launch-type expansion links (one loco built, LMS No 4767, and preserved). Double blastpipe, chimney (replaced with a single version in 1953) and electric lighting which was later removed. Coupled wheelbase 7ft+8ft 4in, total wheelbase 53ft 6¾in. Loco and tender length over buffers 63ft 11¾in. The two mechanical lubricators were driven by a rod attached to the rear end of the back-gear eccentric rod. I section coupling and driving rods.

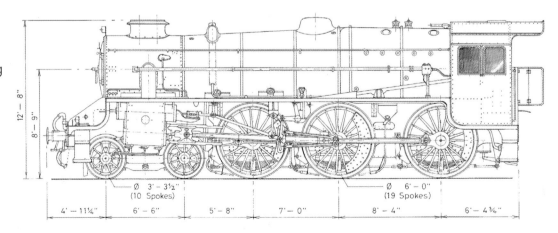

## Stanier Black Fives –
### Listed by introduction date (BR Numbers)

### 1934
45020–45065  August–December, 46 locos built at Vulcan Foundry.

### 1935
45066–45069  January, 4 locos built at Vulcan Foundry.
45000–45019  February–May, 20 locos built at Crewe Works.
45070–45074  February–May, 5 locos built at Crewe Works.
45075–45124  February–July, 50 locos built at Vulcan Foundry.
45125–45224  May–December, 100 locos built at Armstrong Whitworth.

### 1936
45225–45298  August–December, 74 locos built at Armstrong Whitworth.

### 1937
45299–45451  January–December, 153 locos built at Armstrong Whitworth.

### 1938
45452–45471  September–December, 20 locos built at Crewe Works.

### 1943
45472–45491  April–December, 20 locos built at Derby Works.

### 1944
45492–45499  January–April, 8 locos built at Derby Works.
44800–44825  May–December, 26 locos built at Derby Works.
44826–44860  July–December, 35 locos built at Crewe Works.

### 1945
44861–44920  January–December, 60 locos built at Crewe Works.
44932–44943  September–December, 12 locos built Horwich Works.

### 1946
44921–44931  January–April, 11 locos built at Crewe Works.
44944–44966  January–August, 23 locos built at Horwich Works.
44967–44981  April–July, 15 locos built at Crewe Works.
44982–44991  September–December, 10 locos built at Horwich Works.

### 1947
44992–44999  January–March, 8 locos built at Horwich Works.
44783–44799  March–October, 17 locos built at Horwich Works.
44758–44764  September–November, 7 locos built at Crewe Works.
44765–44766  December, 2 locos built at Crewe Works.
44767        December, 1 loco built at Crewe Works.
44768–44782  April–August, 15 locos built at Crewe Works.

### 1948*
44738–44747  June–July, 10 locos built at Crewe Works.
44748–44754  February–April, 7 locos built at Crewe Works.
44755–44757  April–December, 3 locos built at Crewe Works.
44698–44717  July–December, 20 locos built at Horwich Works.

### 1949
44728–44737  January–March, 10 locos built at Crewe Works.
44718–44727  March–May, 10 locos built at Crewe Works.
44658–44667  May–July, 10 locos built at Crewe Works.
44668–44669  December, 2 locos built at Horwich Works.

### 1950
44670–44677  January–April, 8 locos built at Horwich Works.
44678–44685  May–August, 8 locos built at Horwich Works.
44688–44697  August–December, 10 locos built at Horwich Works.

### 1951
44686–44687  April–May, 2 locos built at Horwich Works.

LMS/BR build totals, Crewe Works-Crw (241) Derby Works-Der (54) Horwich Works-Hor (120)

Contractors build totals, Vulcan Foundry-VF (100) Armstrong Whitworth-AW (327)

Class total 842 locomotives. *BR from 1 January 1948.

Note. *Shed Codes used in image and locomotive withdrawal information are those appropriate to the dates stated.*

Two work-stained Stanier 'Black 5s' 4-6-0s, simmer inside Newton Heath motive power depot (9D) in 1967. *Gordon Edgar Collection/Rail Photoprints*

# CHAPTER 2

# 1934

## 45020–45065 August–December, 46 locomotives built at Vulcan Foundry
Introduced with Domeless Boilers, Vertical Throatplates and 14 element Superheaters, locomotive wheelbase 27ft 2in.

### LMS

The London Midland & Scottish Railway (LMS–LMSR) was formed on 1 January 1923 under the Railways Act of 1921.

The LMS had what many considered to be the most logical system of locomotive numbering. All classes were numbered in groups and where possible locomotives of the pre-grouping companies were numbered together. Note the domed boiler and top feed, with the water delivery pipe located on the outside of the boiler cladding. The cabside number is in the high position once favoured by St. Rollox Works, Glasgow with the power rating number 5 located below, note also the location bracket for fitting single line working tablet equipment. This Vulcan Foundry built locomotive (Works Number 4568) entered traffic during August 1934 and was one of the examples initially fitted with a domeless boiler. The first 50 of that build were subsequently re-fitted with domes/domed boilers in the late 1930s. The majority of the first batch of Vulcan Foundry built engines originally had long chimneys and consequently a height of 12ft 10½in above the rails. The chimneys were later changed to match a shorter Crewe pattern thus reducing the above rail height to 12ft 8in; which became the standard for the class. All of the Superheated boilers fitted to the Stanier 'Class 5' engines throughout their working lives were classified as LMS type '3B', despite the several variations in design. Note also the earlier flat profile coupling rods and I section connecting rods. All of the 'Black Five' locomotives were coupled with Stanier 4000 gallon water/9 ton coal tender tanks and the 1932 built Vulcan Foundry tender tanks, locomotives (LMS Nos 5000–5065/BR 45000–45065) were of an all riveted construction. Changes of tenders within the class were made at times, but it seems that a high proportion of the 842 locomotives kept the same tenders throughout their working lives.

Stanier 'Black Five' LMS No 5023, then a Scottish based engine seen in the Manchester area circa 1945. *Mike Morant Collection*

Stanier 'Black Five' BR No 45023 then allocated to Dalry Road (64C) is seen passing Craigleith on the Leith North to Edinburgh Branch with a freight working on 17 May 1955. The fireman has made sure that he can be seen! The Stanier 'Class 5' 4-6-0 was then fitted with a domeless boiler, for a comparison see previous 1945 image of this engine. The locomotives two mechanical lubricators, driven from the top of the right-hand combination lever, are mounted together on the right hand side running board. The LMS original flat style coupling rods with I section connecting rods can also be seen. At that time the locomotive was coupled with a Stanier welded construction lined out tender, with the early style BR logo (so called 'Lion on a Bike'). Note the BR Black livery including lined out cab side with the number in a central position, and the 5 power rating number above it. The 'E 8' trip working indicator plate on the nearside front lamp bracket in this instance, signified a daily working from the port of Granton to Slateford Junction. *David Anderson*

This Vulcan Foundry built locomotive (Works Number 4568) entered service in August 1934 as LMS 5023. After spending the biggest part of its 29 years and 1 month working life allocated to Scottish depots, it was withdrawn from Dalry Road on 30 September 1963 and cut up by Barnes & Bell of Coatbridge in early 1964.

Stanier 'Black Five' BR No 45025 (a preserved example) approaches Preston with a Blackpool – Manchester parcels train, on 10 April 1968. The locomotive was at that time carrying a Carnforth (10A) shedplate. The impressive building alongside the railway is the Roman Catholic Church of St. Walburge, situated on Weston Street, Preston and the square tower has a spire mounted on the top of it. The church was built in the mid-19th century by the Gothic revival architect Joseph Hansom, designer of the 'Hansom Cab', and is famous as having the tallest spire of any parish church in England (309 ft – 94mtrs). Note also the allotments on the trackside bank to the right of the train. *Hugh Ballantyne/Rail Photoprints*

This Vulcan Foundry built locomotive (Works Number 4570) entered traffic during August 1934 as LMS 5025 and was withdrawn from Carnforth depot in August 1968. Thus completing 34 years in LMS/BR revenue earning service. On 13 October 1939 this locomotive was involved in a fatal collision at Bletchley station and severely damaged. It was piloting 'Royal Scot' LMS No 6130 THE WEST YORKSHIRE REGIMENT on a Euston – Stranraer express, it was later repaired and returned to service. BR No 45025 is the oldest of the class in preservation, in 2018 it was based at the Strathspey Steam Railway. As preserved this example was fitted with a 21-element domeless boiler and vertical throatplate. For more information see https://www.strathspeyrailway.co.uk/

Stanier 'Black Five' BR No 45034 then allocated to Monument Lane (3E) is seen piloting 'Jubilee' class BR No 45736 PHEONIX on 'The Midlander', near Rugby on 31 July 1959. In a noticeable departure from the GWR practice to which he was accustomed, Stanier agreed that the 18½in x 28in cylinders of the 'Class 5' engines should be set at a slope, the chosen inclination being 1 in 24. That feature can clearly be seen in this image (likewise on the 'Jubilee' class engine coupled inside). Note also the AWS reservoir cylinder (tank) which is located on the running board between the mechanical lubricators and the cab front. Note the Walschaerts valve gear. 'The Midlander' ran between Euston and Wolverhampton High Level between 1950 and 1959. The inaugural title run took place on 25 September 1950, and the final titled run took place on 11 September 1959. *Mike Morant Collection*

This Vulcan Foundry built locomotive (Works Number 4579) entered traffic during September 1934 as LMS No 5034 and was withdrawn from Speke Junction (8C) in February 1968. After a working life of 33 years and 3 months it was cut up by T.W.Ward of Killamarsh, Yorkshire during May 1968.

## Walschaerts valve gear

Stanier 'Black Five' locomotives, with the exception of BR Nos 44686–44687 (outside Caprotti), 44738–44757 (inside Caprotti) and 44767 (outside Stephenson) were all fitted with Walschaerts valve gear. That system was invented by Belgium railway engineer Egide Walschaerts in 1844. It was extensively used in steam locomotives from the late 19th century until the end of the steam era.

Stanier 'Black Five' as BR No 45039 then allocated to Edge Hill (8A) is seen climbing effortlessly on its way to Shap summit, whilst passing Shap Wells in March 1963. Shap Summit, is the highest point on the WCML from London to Glasgow, at 914ft (278.6 mtrs) above sea level. *Gordon Edgar Collection/Rail Photoprints*

This Vulcan Foundry built locomotive (Works Number 4584) entered traffic during October 1934 as LMS No 5039 and was withdrawn from Edge Hill in August 1967. After a working life of 32 years, 10 months and 1day it was cut up by J. Buttigiegs of Newport during March 1968.

Sister Stanier 'Black Five' locomotives at work, both locomotives are displaying Mold Junction (6B) shedplates.

**Left:** BR No 45042 runs through Warrington Bank Quay station with a down fitted freight, during 1960. Warrington Bank Quay is a north–south orientated station located on the WCML and originally opened by the London & North Western Railway (LNWR) in 1868. *Alan H. Bryant ARPS/Rail Photoprints Collection*

**Right:** BR No 45043 passes Scout Green Signal Box with a down fitted freight on 11 August 1962, with LMS Fowler 2-6-4T BR No 42415 assisting at the rear. Scout Green Signal Box was located on the WCML between Tebay (where banking locomotives could be attached) and Shap summit. The former Saxby & Farmer lever framed signal box was removed during the 1973 electrification and re-signalling project. The first signal box at Scout Green was opened in 1871. *Hugh Ballantyne/Rail Photoprints*

Both locomotives, built by Vulcan Foundry entered traffic during October 1934 as LMS 5042 and 5043 respectively. BR No 45042 (Works Number 4587) was withdrawn from Crewe South (5B) in September 1967, after a working life of 31 years, 11 months and 1 day, and cut up by Cashmores of Great Bridge during December 1967, whilst No 45043 (Works Number 4588) was withdrawn in November 1967 after a working life of 32 years, 1 month and 1 day from Speke Junction (8C) and cut up by Drapers of Hull during February 1968.

Stanier 'Black Five' BR No 45046 then allocated to Crewe South (5B) is seen on the WCML with a Glasgow–Birmingham service circa 1964. Note the overhead power warning plate on the firebox just below the safety valves and the trackside enthusiast. *David Anderson*

Stanier 'Black Five' BR No 45046 (LMS 5046) is this time seen leaning into Didcott East Curve with an up relief comprising of BR Southern Region stock, on 19 June 1965. *David Anderson*

This Vulcan Foundry built locomotive (Works Number 4591) entered traffic in October 1934 as LMS 5046 and was withdrawn from Bolton (9K) in June 1968. After a working life of 32 years, 8 months and 1 day was cut up by Cohens of Kettering during November 1968.

Stanier 'Black Five' BR No 45048 then allocated to Crewe North (5A) is seen leaving the city of Chester with service 1D12 for the North Wales Coast and Holyhead, in July 1964. Stanier 'Black Fives' were a popular and common sight on the North Wales Coast route almost until the end of the steam era. *J.R. Carter/Rail Photoprints Collection*

This Vulcan Foundry built locomotive (Works Number 4593) entered traffic during October 1935 as LMS No 5048 and was withdrawn from Springs Branch (8F) in February 1968. After a working life of 32 years, 1 months and 1 day it was cut up by Drapers of Hull during February 1968.

Stanier 'Black Five' BR No 45050 at Chester General station with a Saturday additional service from North Wales, circa August 1965. The 'Class 5' was then a Stoke (5D) allocated engine.

Stanier 'Black Five' BR No 45050 is again seen at Chester during August 1965. The locomotive is posed with a Manchester train beneath a superb array of ex LNWR lower quadrant signals. In the distance, the imposing structure of Chester No 2 Signal Box (which was demolished in the summer of 1984) can be seen. Note also that the lady in the third carriage window has gone to great lengths to obscure her face from the camera! *Both images Colin Whitfield/Rail Photoprints*

This Vulcan Foundry built locomotive (Works Number 4595) entered traffic during November 1934 as LMS No 5050 and was withdrawn from Stoke (5D) in October 1967. After a working life of 31 years and 9 months it was cut up by Cohens of Kettering in February 1968.

Stanier 'Black Five' BR No 45052 then allocated to Monument Lane (3E) is seen picking up water from Moore Troughs (WCML) as it heads south with a 'City of Birmingham Holiday Express', returning to Birmingham from Southport, on 6 August 1959. Water troughs enabled a locomotive to take water whilst on the move. Although designed and installed for steam locomotives, they were also used by diesel locomotives to replenish their steam heating boilers. Troughs were laid between the rails and were typically a little over a quarter mile long; a scoop on the locomotives was lowered into them where the train's movement caused sufficient pressure to force the water up and into the locomotive's tank. Passengers nearest the locomotive would be wise not to put their heads out of the window whilst the scoop was in use! Moore troughs were each a little over 506 yards in length. *R. A. Whitfield/Rail Photoprints Collection*

This Vulcan Foundry built locomotive (Works Number 4597) entered traffic during November 1934 as LMS 5052 and was withdrawn from Crewe South (5B) in September 1967. After a working life of 31 years and 10 months it was cut up by Cashmores of Great Bridge in February 1968.

Stanier 'Black Five' LMS No 5052 (BR 45052) is seen minus a tender when ex works at Crewe. The locomotive in front of the 'Class 5' is a Bowen Cooke G2A 'Super D' 0-8-0 LMS No 9084 which was built at Crewe in 1910 and withdrawn by BR in 1949 without ever receiving its BR number. After diligent research Vic Smith has dated this image as late August 1936 after discovering that No 5052 was in the works from 18 July 1936 to 18 August 1936 on the occasion of a Heavy General overhaul. *Mike Morant Collection*

As previously stated the combination of flat profile coupling rods and I section driving rods in use at that time can clearly be seen, also from this angle the 1 in 24 inclination of the cylinder casting and associated Walschaert valve gear is obvious. This domeless boiler has a top feed for which the feed water supply pipe is located (and clearly visible) on the outside of the boiler cladding. In this livery style, the then new 'Sans' cabside number is placed horizontally central with the power rating information placed above, and in line with the window mullion thus **5P/ 5F** (**5P**assenger – **5F**reight).

Stanier 'Black Five' BR No 45053 then allocated to St. Margarets (64A) is seen on empty coaching stock duties (ECS) at Edinburgh Waverley station, on 15 July 1966. Note the member of station staff cleaning the carriage windows of coach No EC24267 in the adjacent platform. Edinburgh Waverley is the principal station serving the Scottish capital and it is the northern terminus of the East Coast Main Line (ECML). *Paul Claxton/Rail Photoprints Collection*

This Vulcan Foundry built locomotive (Works Number 4598) entered traffic in November 1934, spending almost all of its working life in Scotland. Withdrawn from Edinburgh St. Margarets during November 1966, after a working life of 31 years it was cut up by Arnott Young of Carmyle during February 1967.

Stanier 'Black Five' LMS No 5055 is seen between duties at Crewe circa 1937 in un-lined LMS livery and with a rivetted tender. LMS No 5055 is seen with a dome plus top feed, and the water delivery pipe is in this instance located under the boiler cladding. *Mike Morant Collection*

This Vulcan Foundry built locomotive (Works Number 4600) entered traffic in November 1934 as LMS 5055 and was withdrawn from Lostock Hall (10D) in February 1968. After a working life of 32 years and 9 months it was cut up by Drapers of Hull during February 1969. The engine was one of the last of the class to be withdrawn.

Stanier 'Black Five' BR No 45056 then allocated to Rugby (2A) looks to be about to commence taking water from Moore troughs as it heads north on the WCML, with 1X91 during August 1963. *R.A. Whitfield/Rail Photoprints*

Stanier 'Black Five' BR No 45056 passes East Croydon with a Brighton bound 1X70 service, circa 1962. Note that the post of the adjacent electric signal is fitted with a white diamond shaped flat metal sign to denote that no signal post telephone is provided, but that a train detained at the signal is protected by a track circuit, of which the controlling signalman is aware (associated with the then requirements of BR Rule 55). *John Day Collection/Rail Photoprints*

This Vulcan Foundry built engine (Works Number 4601) entered traffic during November 1934 as LMS No 5056 and was withdrawn from Speke Junction (8C) in April 1967. After a working life of 31 years and 9 months it was cut up by J. Buttigiegs of Newport during December 1967.

Stanier 'Black Five' BR No 45061 then allocated to Carlisle Kingmoor (12A) is seen northbound on Dillicar Troughs, with a fitted freight, in September 1965. Dillicar (Tebay) had water troughs of differing lengths, the up troughs were 554 yards long and the down 503 yards. The water troughs had to be sited between dead level sections of track. The optimum speed at which to collect water was calculated as being 45mph. However, railway regulations limited trains to 70mph (75mph on the WCML) whilst passing over troughs, irrespective of whether they were taking water or not. *Hugh Ballantyne/Rail Photoprints*

This Vulcan Foundry built locomotive (Works Number 4606) entered traffic during December 1934 as LMS No 5061 and was withdrawn from Carlisle Kingmoor (12A) during November 1967. After a working life of 31 years, 11 months and 1 day it was cut up by Motherwell Machinery & Scrap of Wishaw during March 1968. Interestingly this was one of the class members loaned to the Southern Region of BR to cover for a temporary withdrawal of 'Merchant Navy' class Pacifics in May/June 1953. Those loaned 'Class 5' engines were BR Nos 45051, 45061, 45130, 45216, 45222, 45223 and 45350.

# 1935

## 45066–45069 January, 4 locomotives built at Vulcan Foundry

Introduced with Domeless Boilers, Vertical Throatplates and 14 element Superheaters, locomotive wheelbase 27ft 2in.

Stanier 'Black Five' BR No 45068 then allocated to Accrington (24A) approaches Bolton from the Blackburn line, in the summer of 1960. Note the domeless boiler. The little girl on the platform is intent on showing the train to her doll.
*Alan H. Bryant ARPS/Rail Photoprints Collection*

This Vulcan Foundry built engine (Works Number 4613) entered traffic as LMS No 5068 in January 1935 and was withdrawn from Warrington Dallam (8B) during December 1965. After a service life of 30 years, 10 months and 30 days it was cut up by Cashmores of Great Bridge during April 1966.

Stanier 'Black Five' BR No 45067 then allocated to Crewe South (5B) is seen northbound on the WCML at Golborne with a fitted freight, circa 1962. Note the domed boiler with top feed and also the ex-Great Central Railway St. Helens branch, crossing the mainline. *Jim Carter/Rail Photoprints Collection*

This Vulcan Foundry built engine (Works Number 4612) entered traffic during January 1935 as LMS No 5067 and was withdrawn from Heaton Mersey (9F) in May 1966. After a service life of 32 years, 8 months and 30 days it was cut up J. Buttigiegs of Newport during May 1968.

## 45000-45019 February–May, 20 locomotives built at Crewe Works

45000–45006 Introduced with Domeless Boilers, Vertical Throatplates and 14 element Superheaters, locomotive wheelbase 27ft 2in.

45007–45019 Introduced with 3-row 21 element Superheaters, locomotive wheelbase 27ft 2in.

Preserved Stanier 'Black Five' LMS No 5000 (BR 45000) is seen at the Severn Valley Railway during 1984. This locomotive is preserved as part of the National Collection, and in 2017 was listed by the National Railway Museum (NRM) as a non-operational static exhibit. This locomotive was to have been the first to be completed, however sister engine LMS No 5020 was outshopped from Vulcan Foundry in August 1934. This no doubt resulted in some embarrassment at Crewe Works, which failed to turn out the class leader until some 7 months later! In preservation LMS No 5000 was seen in mainline action on several occasions during the 1980s. *Keith Langston Collection*

For more information visit www.nrm.org.uk/

This Crewe Works built locomotive (Works Number 216) entered traffic during March 1935 as LMS No 5000 and was withdrawn from Lostock Hall (10D) in May 1967, after an LMS/BR service life of 32 years, 7 months and 2 days for preservation. This locomotive was preserved with a Domeless Boiler, Vertical Throatplate and 21 element Superheater.

The very grimy Stanier 'Black Five' BR No 45000 is seen on shed at Wigan Central (27D) during 1960. The engine appears to be coupled to an all welded tender. Note also that the AWS reservoir is in this instance located horizontally to the nearside cab front. *Rail Photoprints Collection*

'Black Five' BR No 45000 takes the Burton Road out of Derby with an up freight, in April 1963. *Rail Photoprints Collection*

On its completion, LMS No 5000 was coupled to tender No 9002 which was especially built with 'roller bearing' axle boxes for the 1933 'Royal Scot' tour of North America. On its return that tender was re-built to the high sided curved top pattern, as were tender Nos 9000/01 originally attached to first two Stanier Pacifics (LMS Nos 6200/6201) and then later attached to 'Black Fives' LMS Nos 5073 and 5074.

Preserved Stanier 'Black Five' LMS No 5000 is seen piloting Severn Valley Railway (SVR) based preserved BR Standard Tank as the pair head the Steam Locomotive Operators Association (S.L.O.A.) 'The Black Countryman' charter past Altrincham North signal box on 19 April 1980. 'The Black Countryman' 1Z77 operated to and from Birmingham New Street being steam hauled by LMS No 5000 and BR No 80079 from Hereford to Manchester Victoria via Church Stretton, Shrewsbury, Wrexham, Chester, Northwich, Altrincham and Guide Bridge. For the return leg, the special was hauled by diesel No 40178 Manchester Victoria to Stockport where electric locomotive No 85013 took over. The planned departure time from Hereford was 11.45 but the actual departure time was recorded as 12.01 making the arrival time in Manchester 18.33 against a planned time of 17.48. *Colin Whitfield/ Rail Photoprints Collection*

Rail tour information from www.sixbellsjunction.co.uk

'Black Five' BR No 45003 then allocated to Crewe North (5A) is seen on shed at Willesden (1A) on 4 June 1961. *Ian Turnbull/Rail Photoprints*

This Crewe Works built locomotive (Works Number 219) entered traffic during April 1935 as LMS No 5003 and was withdrawn from Stoke (5D) in June 1961. After a working life of 32 years and 2 months it was cut up by Cohens of Kettering during Feb 1968.

'Black Five' BR No 45006 then allocated to Trafford Park (9E) is seen outside Crewe Works in 1955, with BR lined black livery and early style emblem. *Rail Photoprints Collection*

This Crewe Works built locomotive (Works Number 222) entered traffic during April 1935 as LMS No 5006 and was withdrawn from Crewe South (5B) in March 1967. After a working life of 32 years and 5 months it was cut up by T. Ward of Killamarsh during December 1967.

Stanier 'Black Five' BR No 45018 then allocated to Carlisle Kingmoor (68A), which was re-branded by British Railways in March 1950, is seen at Inverness, circa 1953. Note that the cabside number is positioned directly under the windows in the style often preferred by the Scottish Region in general and in particular by Glasgow, St. Rollox Works. *Mike Morant Collection*

This Crewe Works built locomotive (Works Number 234) entered traffic during May 1935 as LMS No 5018 and was withdrawn from Carlisle Kingmoor (then 12A) in December 1966. After a working life of 31 years and 7 months it was cut up by Drapers of Hull during June 1967. After being withdrawn from traffic this locomotive was used as a stationary boiler at Eastfield shed (65A) for a short period.

## 45070-45074 February–May, 5 locomotives built at Crewe Works
Introduced with Domeless Boilers, Vertical Throatplates and 21 element Superheaters, locomotive wheelbase 27ft 2in.

Stanier 'Black Five' LMS No 5071 (BR number 45071) in original LMS livery and carrying a Canklow (19C) shedplate, is seen in as built condition passing Elstree with a St. Pancras-Manchester service, during the early summer of 1939. *R. L. Coles (Dave Cobbe Collection)/Rail Photoprints*

This Crewe Works built locomotive (Works Number 237) entered traffic during May 1935 as LMS No 5071 and was withdrawn from Speke Junction (8C) in July 1967. After a working life of 32 years and 2 months it was cut up by Cohens of Kettering during August 1968.

## 45075–45124 February–July, 50 locomotives built at Vulcan Foundry
Introduced with Domeless Boilers, Vertical Throatplates and 21 element Superheaters, locomotive wheelbase 27ft 2in.

Leeds Holbeck (55A) allocated Stanier 'Black Five' BR No 45079, then with a top feed and domed boiler, pulls away from Preston with a service for Manchester Victoria whilst to the right Stanier '4P' 2-6-4T BR No 42546 awaits its next duty as station pilot, September 1965. *Paul Claxton/Rail Photoprints Collection*

This Vulcan Foundry built locomotive (Works Number 4622) entered traffic during March 1935 as LMS No 5079 and was withdrawn from Holbeck (55A) in March 1967. After a working life of 32 years it was cut up by Drapers of Hull during September 1967.

Motherwell (66B) allocated Stanier 'Black Five' BR No 45085, with a top feed only boiler, is seen hard at work near Harthope whilst climbing Beattock Bank with a down freight on 15 August 1955. *David Anderson*

This Vulcan Foundry built locomotive (Works Number 4628) entered traffic during March 1935 as LMS No 5085 and was withdrawn from Motherwell in December 1962 after a working life of 27 years, 10 months and 1 day. It was cut up by Motherwell Machinery & Scrap of Wishaw during November 1963. This locomotive was based in Scotland for the whole of its BR working life.

Preserved Stanier 'Black Five' BR No 45110 (with Domeless boiler, Straight Throatplate and 21 element Superheater) is seen between turns at Bewdley on the Severn Valley Railway, September 2003, note the Holyhead (6J) shedplate. This locomotive was never named in LMS/BR service but for a period in preservation carried the name R.A.F. BIGGIN HILL. BR No 45110 was earmarked directly out of service for preservation and was purchased by David Porter of the 'Flairavia Flying Club' at Biggin Hill Airport. It then moved temporarily to the former BR Ashford shed, and subsequently to the Severn Valley Railway in 1970. The engine was then bought by the SVR, BR No 45110 underwent a major overhaul in their workshops between 1994 and 1998 (returned to service on 11 August 1998). The engine was at that time main line registered, and did haul several main line steam specials on the national rail network. In 2018 the locomotive was reported as being on display at the SVR. *Keith Langston Collection.*

Visit http://www.svr.co.uk/

This Vulcan Foundry built locomotive (Works Number 4653) entered traffic during June 1935 as LMS No 5110 and was withdrawn from Lostock Hall (24C) in August 1968 after a working life of 33 years and 2 months.

Preserved Stanier 'Black Five' BR No 45110 is seen during a 'Last Day of BR Steam' 1Z49 recreation at Northwood Lane on the Severn Valley Railway, 21 September 2003. Note the (6J) Holyhead shedplate. The locomotive was one of three members of the class to haul the 'Fifteen Guinea Special', British Railways' last steam-hauled passenger train, on 11 August 1968. It took the first leg from Liverpool Lime Street to Manchester Victoria at the beginning of the tour before running from Manchester Victoria to Liverpool Lime Street with the returning train later that day. *Fred Kerr*

Stanier 'Black Five' BR No 45111 then allocated to Chester MR (6A) rolls into Rhyl station with the 10.14 Bangor–Manchester Exchange '1K06' service on 7 August 1965, at that time the locomotive was seen with a top feed and domed boiler. Note the impressive structure of 'Rhyl No 2 Signal Box' an ex LNWR Saxby & Farmer type 4 design (127 lever frame). Opened in 1884 the box is of the same class and size as the massive Shrewsbury 'Severn Bridge Junction' box, also built by LNWR in 1903 (and now the largest surviving working mechanical box on BR). The Rhyl box was closed in 1990 and subsequently given listed building status, as it was formerly the largest operational signal box in North Wales. *Ian Turnbull/Rail Photoprints*

This Vulcan Foundry built locomotive (Works Number 4654) entered traffic during June 1935 as LMS No 5111 and was withdrawn from Rose Grove (10F) in August 1966 after a working life of 32 years, 3 months and 30 days. It was cut up by J. Buttigiegs of Newport during May 1968.

## 45125-45224 May–December, 100 locomotives built at Armstrong Whitworth
Introduced with Domeless boilers, Vertical Throatplates and 21 element Superheaters, locomotive wheelbase 27ft 2in.

Stanier 'Black Five' BR No 45126 allocated to Carlisle Kingmoor (68A) on Royal Train duty in Scotland. On 3 July 1956, the Royal Train is seen on the approach to Edinburgh Princes Street station, having travelled via Carlisle (WCML). Note the 4 lamps carried, 3 on the buffer beam and one on the smokebox top lamp bracket of the leading locomotive. The four-lamp code was traditionally used to indicate that the Monarch was on board at that time. Armstrong Whitworth (1935) built BR No 45126 is double heading with class mate BR No 45364, also Armstrong Whitworth built (1937). Two distinctly different boiler designs can be seen, in this image No 45126 has a top feed domeless boiler whilst No 45364 has a top feed and dome. Note that both drivers are making sure they are in the picture. *David Anderson*

Stanier 'Black Five' BR No 45126, fitted with a snow plough and minus its shedplate is seen at Carlisle Kingmoor (68A) on 26 March 1967. Seen by the coaling plant the AW built locomotive is in the company of an unidentified BR Standard Pacific. *Rail Photoprints Collection*

This Armstrong Whitworth built locomotive (Works Number 1167) entered traffic during May 1935 as LMS No 5126 and was withdrawn from Carlisle Kingmoor (68A formerly 12A) in May 1967 where it had spent all of its BR working life, which totalled 32 years. It was cut up by J. McWilliams of Shettleston during November 1967.

Stanier 'Black Five' BR No 45135 then allocated to Carlisle Kingmoor (12A) is seen passing Selside signal box on the Settle–Carlisle route, light engine, on 27 August 1967. The 4-lever signal box was relocated to the site of the former Steam Town Carnforth railway centre in 2008 and although in 2017 it was reported as being in a 'poor state of repair' it is nevertheless a listed building. The former Selside signal box was listed at Grade II for the following principal reasons: Representative: a good example of a Midland Railway (MR) signal box; Rarity: a rare survivor of a very small signal box. *Chris Davies/Rail Photoprints Collection*

This Armstrong Whitworth built locomotive (Works Number 1176) entered traffic during May 1935 as LMS No 5135 and was withdrawn from Carlisle Kingmoor in October 1967 after a working life of 32 years and 5 months. It was cut up by J. McWilliams of Shettleston during March 1968.

Stanier 'Black Five' BR No 45136, then a Perth (63A) allocated locomotive, is seen passing Robroyston with an eight-coach express passenger train for Glasgow (Buchanan Street) on 4 July 1964. Note the local coal merchants yard to the right of the train. *J & J Collection – Sid Rickard/Rail Photoprints*

This Armstrong Whitworth built locomotive (Works Number 1177) entered traffic during May 1935 as LMS No 5136 and was withdrawn from Perth South in October 1964 after a working life of 29 years and 5 months. Having spent all of its BR period in Scotland the locomotive was cut up by Motherwell Machinery & Scrap of Wishaw during February 1965.

Stanier 'Black Five' BR No 45141, displaying a Barrow in Furness (12E) shedplate is seen passing Frodsham with an excursion for North Wales in this delightful 1962 image. *R. A. Whitfield/Rail Photoprints Collection*

This Armstrong Whitworth built locomotive (Works Number 1182) entered traffic during June 1935 as LMS No 5141 and was withdrawn from Lostock Hall (10D) in March 1967 after a working life of 31 years 8 months and 28 days. It was cut up by J. McWilliams of Shettleston during September 1967.

Stanier 'Black Five' BR No 45145 then allocated to Crewe South (5B) with a Manchester bound service stands on the Weaver Bridge at Frodsham waiting for the signal, circa 1965. *Colin Whitfield/Rail Photoprints*

This Armstrong Whitworth built locomotive (Works Number 1186) entered traffic during June 1935 as LMS No 5145 and was withdrawn from Crewe South in November 1967 after a working life of 32 years and 5 months. It was cut up by Cashmores of Great Bridge during February 1968.

Stanier 'Black Five' BR No 45151, displaying a Motherwell (66B) shedplate is seen nearing the summit of Beattock Bank on 17 August 1955 with a down freight for Motherwell/Glasgow, whilst being assisted at the rear by LMS (CR) Class '439' 0-4-4T BR No 55260. Interestingly at that time this example was fitted with a domed boiler with a top feed located on the front ring of the boiler barrel. *David Anderson*

This Armstrong Whitworth built locomotive (Works Number 1192) entered traffic during June 1935 as LMS No 5151 and was withdrawn from Motherwell in December 1962 after a working life of 27 years, 6 months and 28 days having spent all its BR period in Scotland. It was cut up by Motherwell Machinery & Scrap of Wishaw during August 1963.

Stanier 'Black Five' BR No 45154 LANARKSHIRE YEOMANRY, then allocated to Newton Heath (26A), is seen at Preston on 1 June 1957. Note the regimental crest on the nameplate. It can be seen that the ECS working information is chalked on the smokebox door. *Rail Photoprints Collection*

This Armstrong Whitworth built locomotive (Works Number 1195) entered traffic during June 1935 as LMS No 5154 and was withdrawn from Speke Junction (8C) in November 1966 after a working life of 31 years and 5 months. It was cut up by Drapers of Hull during May 1967.

Stanier 'Black Five' BR No 45156 AYRSHIRE YEOMANRY is seen at its then home shed Dalry Road (64C) Edinburgh in 1954. Note the domed boiler. *David Anderson*

Replica nameplate.

This Armstrong Whitworth built locomotive (Works Number 1197) entered traffic during July 1935 as LMS No 5156 and was withdrawn from Rose Grove (10F) in August 1968 (coinciding with the end of BR steam) after a working life of 33 years, 1 month and 1 day. It was cut up by T. W. Ward of Sheffield during December 1968.

Stanier 'Black Five' BR No 45156 AYRSHIRE YEOMANRY, then allocated to Newton Heath 26A, passes Manchester Victoria with an empty coaching stock working (ECS), comprised mainly of Eastern Region vehicles circa 1960. Note that in this later image the locomotive has been fitted with a domeless boiler (see previous image for comparison). *Alan H Bryant ARPS/Rail Photoprints*

Stanier 'Black Five' BR No 45156 is seen minus nameplates (AYRSHIRE YEOMANRY) whilst under the coaling plant at Carnforth (then 10A) during the last month of BR steam operation, 4 August 1968. Note the St. Rollox shed plate (65B) an acknowledgement to the engines 1948 allocation. *A W Nokes/Rail Photoprints*

A Stockport (Bahamas) Locomotive Society board is carried on the buffer beam. This 'Farewell to Steam' 4/08/68 rail tour (one of five so named tours on that day) was actually listed as being run by G.C. Enterprises as 'IT80'. The published route being Stockport-Manchester-Bolton-Blackburn-Hellifield-Carnforth and return. For rail tour information visit www.sixbellsjunction.co.uk

Stanier 'Black Five' LMS No 45157 THE GLASGOW HIGHLANDER, a St. Rollox (65B) allocated engine, is seen passing Robroyston with the 11.15am Glasgow (Buchanan Street)–Dundee (West) express on 7 October 1961. *J & J Collection – Sid Rickard/Rail Photo Prints*

Preserved Stanier 'Black Five' BR No 45407 is seen masquerading as No 45157 THE GLASGOW HIGHLANDER at the 2003 Crewe Works Open Day. *Keith Langston Collection*

This Armstrong Whitworth built locomotive (Works Number 1198) entered traffic during July 1935 as LMS No 5157 and was withdrawn from St. Rollox in December 1962 after having spent all of the BR steam era at that shed. After a working life of 27 years, 5 months and 29 days it was cut up by Arnott Young of Troon during July 1963.

Stanier 'Black Five' BR No 45158 GLASGOW YEOMANRY then allocated to St. Rollox (65B), with snow plough stands at Callander station whilst at the head of an Oban – Glasgow service, on 3 April 1961. Note the snow on the high tops and the postman waiting for the mail, his van can be seen on the car park *J & J Collection - Sid Rickard/Rail Photoprints*

This Armstrong Whitworth built locomotive (Works Number 1199) entered traffic during July 1935 as LMS No 5158 and was withdrawn from Dumfries (67E) in July 1964 after having spent all of the BR steam era allocated to Scottish sheds. After a working life of 29 years it was cut up by Arnott Young of Troon during October 1964.

Stanier 'Black Five' BR No 45158 GLASGOW YEOMANRY, is seen on the turntable with the locomotive crew and a yard worker in attendance, the location is thought to be St. Rollox. The nameplate with regimental crest is clearly seen as is the single line tablet equipment mounted on the cab side under the number. Note also the early BR 'Lion on a Bike' emblem on the full tender in this busy March 1959 image. *Rail Photoprints Collection*

Stanier 'Black Five' BR No 45168 then allocated to Dalry Road (64C) reverses out of Lanark with the ECS from an earlier Carstairs arrival. The train will be turned on the triangle before the return departure, 21 September 1963. *J & J Collection – Sid Rickard/Rail Photoprints*

This Armstrong Whitworth built locomotive (Works Number 1209) entered traffic during August 1935 as LMS No 5168 and was withdrawn from Edinburgh St. Margarets (64A) in September 1966 after having spent all of the BR steam era allocated to Scottish sheds. After a working life of 31 years and 1 month it was cut up by J. McWilliams of Shettleston during January 1967.

Stanier 'Black Five' BR No 45171 then allocated to Corkerhill (67A) pilots 'Jubilee' BR No 45608 GIBRALTER as they prepare to leave Glasgow St. Enoch with the 08.45 relief service to London St. Pancras on 30 March 1964. Glasgow St. Enoch station was closed on 27 June 1966 as part of the rationalisation of the railway system undertaken by the British Railways Board Chairman Dr. Richard Beeching. The structure and the hotel that fronted it were demolished in 1977. The clock that was suspended from the roof of the station was saved from destruction and is now on display in Cumbernauld Town Centre. *Ian Turnbull/Rail Photoprints Collection*

This Armstrong Whitworth built locomotive (Works Number 1212) entered traffic during August 1935 as LMS No 5171 and was withdrawn from Carstairs (66E) in October 1965 after having spent all of the BR steam era allocated to Scottish sheds. After a working life of 30 years, 1 month and 30 days it was cut up by Motherwell Machinery & Scrap of Wishaw during February 1966.

Stanier 'Black Five' BR No 45172 then allocated to Polmadie (66A) is seen with a Creative Tourist Agent's Conference (CTAC) special train at speed near Symington on the West Coast Mainline on 25 June 1960. The Creative Tourist Agent's Conference was a consortium of nine UK travel agents and firms which chartered special trains in the periods 1933-1939 and 1945-1968. *David Anderson*

This Armstrong Whitworth built locomotive (Works Number 1213) entered traffic during August 1935 as LMS No 5172 and was withdrawn from Carstairs (66E) in May 1964 after having spent all of the BR steam era allocated to Scottish sheds. After a working life of 28 years, 8 months and 30 days it was cut up by Connels of Coatbridge during September 1964.

Stanier 'Black Five' BR No 45176 is seen departing Beattock with a down passenger service on 8 September 1958. Note that the then Motherwell allocated (66B) locomotive has blue backed smokebox door number and shed plates. *David Anderson*

This Armstrong Whitworth built locomotive (Works Number 1217) entered traffic during August 1935 as LMS No 5176 and was withdrawn from Motherwell in May 1964 after having spent all of the BR steam era allocated to that depot. After a working life of 31 years it was cut up by Motherwell Machinery & Scrap of Wishaw during November 1966.

Stanier 'Black Five' BR No 45178 then allocated to St. Rollox (65B) gets the single line section token as it passes Glenogle passing loop with an Oban–Glasgow service on 22 August 1960. *Hugh Ballantyne/ Rail Photoprints*

This Armstrong Whitworth built locomotive (Works Number 1219) entered traffic during September 1935 as LMS No 5178 and was withdrawn from Motherwell (66B) in January 1965 after having spent all of the BR steam era allocated to Scottish depots. After a working life of 29 years and 4 months it was cut up by Motherwell Machinery & Scrap of Wishaw during May 1965.

Stanier 'Black Five' BR No 45183 displaying a Dalry Road (64C) shedplate is about to depart Stirling station with the 10.15 am working to Edinburgh Princes Street station in September 1964. Note the Dalry Road shed name stencilled on the buffer beam. *David Anderson*

This Armstrong Whitworth built locomotive (Works Number 1224) entered traffic during September 1935 as LMS No 5183 and was withdrawn from Dalry Road in October 1964. After a working life of 29 years and 30 days it was cut up by Motherwell Machinery & Scrap of Wishaw during March 1965.

Stanier 'Black Five' BR No 45193 then allocated to Carnforth (10A) works hard with a northbound freight at Lambrigg Crossing, on 25 January 1967. *Paul Claxton/Rail Photoprints Collection*

This Armstrong Whitworth built locomotive (Works Number 1234) entered traffic during October 1935 as LMS No 5193 and was withdrawn from Carnforth in August 1967. After a working life of 31 years, 10 months and 1 day it was cut up by Cashmores of Great Bridge during March 1968.

Stanier 'Black Five' BR No 45194 an Ayr (67C) allocated locomotive passes Ayr Harbour Junction with coal trucks for Ayr Harbour, on 23 June 1961. *J & J Collection – Sid Rickard/Rail Photoprints*

This Armstrong Whitworth built locomotive (Works Number 1235) entered traffic during October 1935 as LMS No 5194 and was withdrawn from Ayr in April 1965 after spending all of the BR steam era in Scotland. After a working life of 29 years, 6 months and 1 day it was cut up by Motherwell Machinery & Scrap of Wishaw during July 1965.

Stanier 'Black Five' BR No 45210 then allocated to Carlisle Kingmoor (12A) is seen near Wallerscote Junction with an up WCML fitted freight, during September 1962. Note the 25KvAC overhead catenary equipment and power lines, accordingly the locomotive carries the prescribed warning signs. *R. A. Whitfield/Rail Photoprints*

This Armstrong Whitworth built locomotive (Works Number 1251) entered traffic during November 1935 as LMS No 5210 and was withdrawn from Carlisle Kingmoor in June 1966. After a working life of 32 years and 7 months it was cut up by Drapers of Hull during October 1968.

Stanier 'Black Five' BR No 45218 then allocated to Southport (27C) heading a Cadbury's special is seen approaching Halton Station, near Frodsham Junction, during April 1962. *R.A. Whitfield/Rail Photoprints*

This Armstrong Whitworth built locomotive (Works Number 1259) entered traffic during November 1935 as LMS No 5218 and was withdrawn from Carlisle Kingmoor (12A) in April 1966. After a working life of 30 years and 5 months it was cut up by J. McWilliams of Shettleston during July 1966.

Stanier 'Black Five' BR No 45219 approaches Sheffield Victoria with 'The South Yorkshireman' circa 1957. 'The South Yorkshireman', London Marylebone-Bradford Exchange via Huddersfield and Halifax, was the first title to be conferred by British Railways (BR). The inaugural titled run was 31 May 1948 and the last titled run 2 January 1960. *Rail Photoprints Collection*

This Armstrong Whitworth built locomotive (Works Number 1260) entered traffic during November 1935 as LMS No 5219 and was withdrawn from Leeds Holbeck MR (55A) in October 1967. After a working life of 31 years, 10 months and 30 days it was cut up by T.W. Ward of Killamarsh during February 1968.

Preserved Stanier 'Black Five' BR No 45212, note the Lostock Hall (10D) shedplate is seen backing down to Grosmont station at the NYMR on the occasion of the Wartime Weekend in 2010. This locomotive was originally introduced with a domeless boiler and 14 element Superheater but was rebuilt with a dome and 24 element Superheater. *Phil Brown*

This Armstrong Whitworth built locomotive (Works Number 1253) entered traffic during November 1935 as LMS No 5212 and was withdrawn from Lostock Hall at the end of the British Railways (BR) steam era on 31 August 1968.

After an LMS/BR working life of 32 years and 9 months it survived into preservation having had the distinction of heading the final steam-hauled revenue-earning service for BR on 4 August 1968. It was bought direct from BR by the Keighley & Worth Valley Railway (KWVR) and arrived there in October 1968. In addition to a successful period in preservation the locomotive also had a major rebuild to mainline operating standard thanks to a unique agreement between the Keighley & Worth Valley Railway and the Bury-based engineering company Riley & Son (E) Ltd. However, in recent years the locomotive has been based at the North Yorkshire Moors Railway (NYMR). For further details visit https://www.nymr.co.uk/

Preserved Stanier 'Black Five' BR No 45212 is seen hard at work on the North Yorkshire Moors Railway climbing out of Newtondale. The glorious Autumn colours of the stunning gorge provide an impressive backdrop. *Phil Brown*

For a period in preservation the locomotive carried the curved cast nameplate ROY 'KORKY' GREEN above a smaller plaque inscribed RAILWAYMAN 1826-2001, both were mounted on a steel plate above the central driving wheel. *Phil Brown*

Stanier 'Black Five' BR No 45222 then allocated to Bletchley (1E) passes through Fenny Stratford Station with a mixed freight bound for Bedford, circa 1962. *A. J. B. Dodd/Rail Photoprints*

This Armstrong Whitworth built locomotive (Works Number 1263) entered traffic during December 1935 as LMS No 5222 and was withdrawn from Newton Heath (9D) in February 1967. After a working life of 31 years, 2 months and 1 day it was cut up by Drapers of Hull during July 1967.

# 1936

## 45225-45298 August-December, 74 locomotives built at Armstrong Whitworth

ntroduced with Domed Boilers, Sloping Throatplates and 24 element Superheaters, locomotive wheelbase 27ft 2in. On 23 January 1955 locomotive BR No 45274 from this batch derailed on a curve at Sutton Coldfield due to excessive speed causing a fatal accident. The engine was returned to service after repair.

Stanier 'Black Five' BR No 45225 is seen in the summer of 1949 shortly after receiving British Railways number and livery, the location is thought to be Bank Hall (23A). Note also sister engine with cabside number LMS M4820, but with the tender lettered in the early BR style. *John Day Collection/Rail Photoprints*

This Armstrong Whitworth built locomotive (Works Number 1280) entered traffic during August 1936 as LMS No 5225 and was withdrawn from Stockport Edgeley (9B) in October 1967. After a working life of 31 years, 1 month and 30 days it was cut up by Cashmores of Newport during July 1968.

Stanier 'Black Five' BR No 45226 then a Lostock Hall (10D) allocated locomotive heads south through Hartford on the West Coast Main Line with an up-passenger service, on 20 August 1966. *Colin Whitfield/Rail Photoprints*

This Armstrong Whitworth built locomotive (Works Number 1281) entered traffic during August 1936 as LMS No 5226 and was withdrawn from Lostock Hall in October 1967. After a working life of 31 years and 1 month it was cut up by Cashmores of Newport during June 1968.

Stanier 'Black Five' BR No 45227 then a Carnforth (10A) allocated locomotive is seen at Leeds City station in 1963. The very wet day has not deterred the two young enthusiasts who appear to have been chatting to the driver, and like him are 'looking for the road'. Note the DMU in the adjacent platform, the planned end of steam was well underway. *Keith Langston Collection*

This Armstrong Whitworth built locomotive (Works Number 1282) entered traffic during August 1936 as LMS No 5227 and was withdrawn from Lostock Hall (10D) in January 1968. After a working life of 31 years and 5 months it was cut up by Drapers of Hull during April 1968.

Stanier 'Black Five' BR No 45230 heads a mixed rake of coal and mineral empties on the outskirts of Todmorden circa 1964. Freight traffic was once the mainstay of the UK's railway network but started to decline steadily in the post war years. Coal and mineral traffic formed a large proportion of those movements, none more so than the coal required for the steam locomotives themselves. *Keith Langston Collection*

This Armstrong Whitworth built locomotive (Works Number 1285) entered traffic during August 1936 as LMS No 5230 and was withdrawn from Carnforth (10A) in August 1965. The locomotive had a working life of approximately 29 years, but scrapping details are uncertain.

Preserved Stanier 'Black Five' BR No 45231 is seen heading 'The Welsh Mountaineer' charter from Preston as it emerges from the tunnel into the slate strewn landscape of Blaenau Ffestiniog on a very wet 26 August 2009. *Gordon Edgar/Rail Photoprints*

In preservation, BR No 45321 has carried both the names 3RD (VOLUNTEER) BATTALION THE WORCESTERSHIRE AND SHERWOOD FORESTERS REGIMENT and THE SHERWOOD FORESTER (as shown above) although it never carried either of these names in LMS or BR service.

This Armstrong Whitworth built locomotive (Works Number 1286) entered traffic during August 1936 as LMS No 5231 and was withdrawn from Carnforth (10A) in August 1968 (at the end of BR steam). After an LMS/BR working life of 32 years it was saved for preservation. As preserved it was fitted with a sloping throatplate, domed boiler, top feed on second ring of boiler barrel and 24 element superheater.

Preserved Stanier 'Black Five' BR No 45231 THE SHERWOOD FORESTER is seen double heading a special charter train with sister 'Black Five' No (4)5407 on the Conwy Valley line at Roman Bridge, en-route for Blaenau Ffestiniog in May 2009. Note the Carnforth (10A) shedplate. *Sue Langston*

Throughout the 1950s and early 1960s the locomotive was allocated to a number of depots across the North West and Midlands. In May 1968 BR No 45231 was transferred to Carnforth (10A) and as a consequence it became one of the locomotives which served BR until the very end of steam. The first restoration took over 10 years to complete with the locomotive returning to steam in 1988, and a year later moving to the Nene Valley Railway remaining there until the 1990s.

The locomotive was purchased by the Great Central Railway in the mid-1990s and at that time it was given the name THE SHERWOOD FORESTER. Changing hands again in 2003, it was purchased by the former professional cyclist Bert Hitchen who had long been involved in locomotive preservation. The engine returned to the main line in 2005 and worked numerous railtours across the country before undergoing another overhaul. In May 2015 Bert Hitchen sadly passed away and shortly after his death locomotive owner Jeremy Hosking purchased the locomotive from the Hitchen family. The Armstrong Whitworth built Stanier 'Black Five' BR No 45231 is now part of the 'Icons of Steam' fleet. See www.iconsofsteam.com

Preserved Stanier 'Black Five' BR No 45231 THE SHERWOOD FORESTER is seen at Deer Leap Wood near Wotton with 'The Cathedrals Express' (reporting number 1Z82) ex Kensington Olympia for Guildford and return on 14 February 2006. *John Chalcraft/ Rail Photoprints*

Preserved Stanier 'Black Five' BR No 45231 THE SHERWOOD FORESTER, complete with a remembrance wreath on the smokebox door is seen passing Rabbit Lane, Great Central Railway (GCR) on Sunday 8 November 2009. *Phil Sangwell*

Stanier 'Black Five' BR No 45233 with a 26A (Newton Heath) shed plate, in the company of sister engine 45054 and an unidentified 2-6-4T, is seen in a freshly painted condition at Crewe Works in this undated BR era image. Note that the locomotives are fully lined and numbered but none have yet received a logo (tender). *Mike Morant Collection*

This Armstrong Whitworth built locomotive (Works Number 1288) entered traffic during August 1936 as LMS No 5233 and was withdrawn from Trafford Park (9E) in May 1966. After a working life of 29 years, 8 months and 30 days it was cut up by Cashmores of Great Bridge during September 1966.

Stanier 'Black Five' BR No 45235 then a Carlisle Kingmoor (12A) allocated locomotive, is seen departing from Paisley (Gilmour Street) Station with the 10.40am Gourock–Glasgow (Central) express passenger train, on 4 January 1965. Note the shed name stencilled on the buffer beam. *J & J Collection – Sid Rickard/Rail Photoprints*

This Armstrong Whitworth built locomotive (Works Number 1290) entered traffic during August 1936 as LMS No 5235 and was withdrawn from Carlisle Kingmoor in January 1966. After a working life of 29 years and 5 months it was cut up by J. McWilliams of Shettleston during April 1966.

Stanier 'Black Five' BR No 45245 then allocated to Carstairs (66E), is seen working hard whilst climbing Beattock Bank with a down Class K freight in September 1962. *J & J Collection – Sid Rickard/Rail Photoprints*

This Armstrong Whitworth built locomotive (Works Number 1300) entered traffic during September 1936 as LMS No 5245 and was withdrawn from Carstairs in August 1965. After a working life of 28 years and 11 months it was cut up by Motherwell Machinery & Scrap of Wishaw during November 1965.

Stanier 'Black Five' BR No 45255 then allocated to Newton Heath (9D) leaves Manchester Exchange with a westbound parcels train on 9 March 1968. *David Rostance Rail/Photoprints Collection*

This Armstrong Whitworth built locomotive (Works Number 1310) entered traffic during October 1936 as LMS No 5255 and was withdrawn from Newton Heath in June 1968. After a working life of 31 years, 8 months and 1 day it was cut up by Drapers of Hull during February 1969.

Stanier 'Black Five' BR No 45261 then allocated to Agecroft (26B) arriving at Wigan Wallgate with the four coach 07.56 Liverpool Exchange – Rochdale service, on 3 June 1963.
*Ian Turnbull/Rail Photoprints*

This Armstrong Whitworth built locomotive (Works Number 1316) entered traffic during October 1936 as LMS No 5261 and was withdrawn from Stockport Edgeley (9B) in October 1967. After a working life of 31 years it was cut up by Cashmores of Newport during February 1968.

Stanier 'Black Five' BR No 45262 then allocated to Sheffield Grimesthorpe (19A) gets smartly away from Chinley with an up-passenger service, circa 1954. Note the tank engine heading the train in the bay platform to the right, the 4-4-0 shunting stock under the covered footbridge to the left and the period advertising bill boards including Belle Vue, Bakewell Show and of course Guinness. *Steve Armitage Archive/Rail Photoprints*

This Armstrong Whitworth built locomotive (Works Number 1317) entered traffic during October 1936 as LMS No 5262 and was withdrawn from Rose Grove (10F) in August 1968. After a working life of 31 years, 10 months and 1 day it was cut up by Cashmores of Newport during September 1968.

Stanier 'Black Five' BR No 45263 then allocated to Saltley (21A) is seen taking water on Moore Troughs whilst heading a City of Leicester holiday special to the Fylde Coast in the summer of 1962. *R.A. Whitfield/Rail Photoprints*

This Armstrong Whitworth built locomotive (Works Number 1318) entered traffic during October 1936 as LMS No 5263 and was withdrawn from Heaton Mersey (9F) in October 1967. After a working life of 31 years it was cut up by Cashmores of Newport during June 1968.

Stanier 'Black Five' BR No 45270 then allocated to Crewe North (5A) approaches Winsford with the 06.15 Carlisle – Crewe, on 3 April 1961. *Hugh Ballantyne/Rail Photoprints*

This Armstrong Whitworth built locomotive (Works Number 1325) entered traffic during November 1936 as LMS No 5270 and was withdrawn from Crewe South (5B) in September 1967. After a working life of 30 years and 10 months it was cut up by Cashmores of Great Bridge during January 1968.

Stanier 'Black Five' BR No 45279 then allocated to Llandudno Junction (6G) is seen leaving Colwyn Bay with the 11.05 service to Liverpool Lime Street, on 7 August 1965. Note the banner repeater standing at the entry to the down platform. Sometimes a signal can be obscured by the landscape, a curve, platform canopy, bridges, or other structures. Each signal should have a minimum sighting distance and if this is not met then a banner repeater can be used to replicate the aspect of the obscured signal. *Ian Turnbull/Rail Photoprints*

This Armstrong Whitworth built locomotive (Works Number 1334) entered traffic during November 1936 as LMS No 5279 and was withdrawn from Heaton Mersey (9F) in March 1968. After a working life of 31 years, 3 months and 29 days it was cut up by Cashmores of Great Bridge during September 1968.

Stanier 'Black Five' BR No 45282 then allocated to Llandudno Junction (6G) in a very smart condition and with recently painted buffers at Patricroft after having been coaled, watered and serviced, in April 1965. *Jim Carter/Rail Photoprints*

This Armstrong Whitworth built locomotive (Works Number 1337) entered traffic during November 1936 as LMS No 5282 and was withdrawn from Edge Hill (8A) in May 1968. After a working life of 31 years, 5 months and 30 days it was cut up by T.W. Ward of Killamarsh during October 1968.

Stanier 'Black Five' BR No 45283 then allocated to Oxley (2B). The locomotive looks to be in a very scruffy condition as it takes water at Aylesbury, the driver on the valve and fireman on the bag. This northbound working on the ex-Great Central section took place on 13 June 1966 just months before cessation of through services. The coal brazier seen behind the water column would have been kept lit in winter to stop the water in the column from freezing. *Rail Photoprints Collection*

This Armstrong Whitworth built locomotive (Works Number 1338) entered traffic during November 1936 as LMS No 5283 and was withdrawn from Oxley in January 1967. After a working life of 30 years and 2 months it was cut up by Cashmores of Great Bridge during May 1967.

Stanier 'Black Five' BR No 45284 then allocated to Edge Hill (8A) is seen in an unloved and work stained condition adjacent to the coaling plant at Patricroft (9H) in October 1963. Note that the shed plate has been removed and the code has been roughly hand painted on to the smokebox door. *R. A. Whitfield/Rail Photoprints*

This Armstrong Whitworth built locomotive (Works Number 1339) entered traffic during December 1936 as LMS No 5284 and was withdrawn from Edge Hill in May 1968. After a working life of 31 years and 5 months it was cut up by T.W. Ward of Killamarsh during August 1968.

Stanier 'Black Five' BR No 45292 then allocated to Llandudno Junction (7A) passes Dunham Hill station with a Llandudno – Manchester service in 1949, whilst the photographer's young son looks on admiringly. Note the Sans insignia (number style) and the words British Railways on the tender. Dunham Hill station (serving Dunham on the Hill, Cheshire) closed in 1952 and the buildings were demolished, the platforms however, remained until the 1970s. *R.A. Whitfield/Rail Photoprints*

This Armstrong Whitworth built locomotive (Works Number 1347) entered traffic during December 1936 as LMS No 5292 and was withdrawn from Birkenhead (8H) in November 1967. After a working life of 30 years, 11 months and 1 day it was cut up by Cashmores of Great bridge during March 1968.

Stanier 'Black Five' BR No 45292 is seen again passing Halton Signal Box in 1949. The box closed in 1967. *R.A. Whitfield/Rail Photoprints*

Stanier 'Black Five' BR No 45292 is once more seen, this time passing Helsby in 1948. *R.A. Whitfield/Rail Photoprints*

# 1937

## 45299-45451 January-December, 153 locomotives built at Armstrong Whitworth

Introduced with Domed Boilers, Sloping Throatplates and 24 element Superheaters, locomotive wheelbase 27ft 2in. In 1941 locomotive BR No 45425 from this batch was severely damaged during a German air raid, it was later repaired at Crewe Works.

Stanier 'Black Five' BR No 45303 then allocated to Warrington Dallam (8B) is seen on the turntable inside Wellingborough shed (15B) on 15 September 1965. *Hugh Ballantyne/ Rail Photoprints*

This Armstrong Whitworth built locomotive (Works Number 1358) entered traffic during January 1937 as LMS No 5303 and was withdrawn from Warrington Dallam (8B) in June 1967. After a working life of 30 years and 5 months it was cut up by Cohens of Kettering during June 1967.

Later to be preserved Stanier 'Black Five' BR No 45305 then carrying Chester (6A) shedplate is seen slowly passing through a semi derelict section of Liverpool's Dockland with 1T85 the Locomotive Club of Great Britain (LCGB) 'Lancastrian' railtour, on 6 April 1968. Note the flagman accompanying the special. The author has fond memories of this rail tour. *Rail Photoprints Collection*

This Armstrong Whitworth built locomotive (Works Number 1360) entered traffic during January 1937 as LMS No 5305 and was withdrawn from Lostock Hall (10D) in August 1968. After a working life of 31 years and 7 months it was saved for preservation with a domed boiler, sloping throatplate, 24 element superheater and a top feed on second ring of boiler barrel.

LMS No 5305 became the last locomotive on the scrap line of Drapers of Hull, who broke up 742 former BR locomotives. No 5305 was to have been the 743rd and last, but it was decided to preserve it and bring it back to full running order.

Albert Draper was, at the time, the president of Hull Kingston Rovers Rugby League Football Club, and it was his fond wish that No 5305 would one-day head a special train from Hull to Wembley, where he hoped the club would be playing in the Rugby League Challenge Cup Final.

To facilitate its restoration No 5305 was put into the care of the Humberside Locomotive Preservation Group and based at the former Hull Dairycoates steam depot (where it was eventually brought up to full main line standard). The locomotive left Hull Dairycoates in April 1992 on the closure of that shed and went into storage at the site of RAF Binbrook in Lincolnshire.

It eventually arrived on the Great Central Railway (GCR) on 20 November, 1996 where it was again returned to steam, in 2003. On 26 April, 2005 the Mayor of Charnwood, Mike Jones, welcomed the Lord Mayor of Hull, John Fareham, to the GCR to re-name the 'Black Five' 'ALDERMAN A E DRAPER' using nameplates which were first used in 1984. The locomotive remains in the ownership of A. E. Draper and Sons and in 2018 was in the long-term care of the '5305 Locomotive Association', the successor to the Humberside Locomotive Preservation Group.

Preserved Stanier 'Black Five' is seen at Ais Gill, on the Settle Carlisle route on 22 March 1980 whilst on 'Cumbrian Mountain Express' duty. *Rail Photoprints Collection*

Stanier 'Black Five' BR No 45312 then a Patricroft (10C) allocated locomotive is seen emerging from Sutton Tunnel 'wrong line' (due to permanent way repairs) as it heads a North Wales bound special, circa 1949. *R. A. Whitfield/Rail Photoprints*

This Armstrong Whitworth built locomotive (Works Number 1367) entered traffic during February 1937 as LMS No 5312 and was withdrawn from Bolton (9K) in June 1967. After a working life of 31 years and 4 months it was cut up by Cohens of Kettering during February 1969.

Stanier 'Black Five' LMS No 45317 then allocated to Crewe South (5B) is seen as LMS No 5317 with a down freight at Low Gill on the WCML. The bridge in the background was demolished and the road re-routed during the construction of the M6 motorway. *Mike Morant Collection*

This Armstrong Whitworth built locomotive (Works Number 1372) entered traffic during February 1937 as LMS No 5317 and was withdrawn from Carlisle Kingmoor (12A) in November 1963. After a working life of 26 years and 9 months it was cut up by Crewe Works during November 1963.

Stanier 'Black Five' BR No 45319 then allocated to Inverness (60A) is seen between turns at Forres, on 31 March 1956, note the buffer beam snowplough and tablet changing equipment on the cab side. *Rail Photoprints Collection*

This Armstrong Whitworth built locomotive (Works Number 1374) entered traffic during February 1937 as LMS No 5319 and was withdrawn from Motherwell (66B) in May 1967. After a working life of 30 years, 2 months and 30 days it was cut up by J. McWilliams of Shettleston during September 1967.

Stanier 'Black Five' BR No 45322 then allocated to Bescot (3A) is seen approaching Weaver Junction (WCML) with a down passenger service, circa 1949. *R.A. Whitfield/Rail Photoprints*

This Armstrong Whitworth built locomotive (Works Number 1377) entered traffic during February 1937 as LMS No 5322 and was withdrawn from Stoke (5D) in September 1966. After a working life of 29 years and 7 months it was cut up by Cashmores of Great Bridge during April 1967.

Stanier 'Black Five' BR No 45327 then allocated to Llandudno Junction (6G) emerges from Sutton Tunnel at Halton with a Manchester–North Wales service during August 1963, note the castellated style of the tunnel mouth. *R.A. Whitfield/Rail Photoprints*

This Armstrong Whitworth built locomotive (Works Number 1382) entered traffic during March 1937 as LMS No 5327 and was withdrawn from Llandudno Junction (6G) in January 1965. After a working life of 27 years, 10 months and 3 days it was cut up by Motherwell Machinery & Scrap of Wishaw during July 1965.

Stanier 'Black Five' BR No 45330 then allocated to Warrington Dallam hurries north through Penrith station with a down express freight bound for Carlisle, on 22 July 1967.
*Chris Davies/Rail Photoprints*

This Armstrong Whitworth built locomotive (Works Number 1385) entered traffic during March 1937 as LMS No 5330 and was withdrawn from Carnforth (10A) in August 1968. After a working life of 31 years, 5 months and 3 days it was cut up by Cohens of Cargo Fleet during December 1968.

Preserved Stanier 'Black Five' BR No 45337 is seen approaching Irwell Vale on the East Lancashire Railway during June 2005. *Fred Kerr*

This Armstrong Whitworth built locomotive (Works Number 1392) entered traffic during April 1937 as LMS No 5337 and was withdrawn from Carlisle Kingmoor (12A) in February 1965. After a working life of 27 years, and 10 months it was preserved, with a domed boiler, sloping throatplate, 28 element superheater and a top feed on the second ring of the boiler barrel.

The locomotive was bought from BR for scrap by Woodham Brothers, Barry in 1965 but fortunately it remained un-cut at that scrapyard until it was purchased and removed for preservation in May 1984. Following a further overhaul, which was completed in September 2010 the locomotive currently has a boiler certificate valid until 2020. This fully restored and much-travelled class member is now owned by the Bury based '26B Railway Company' who on a commercial basis loan the 'Black Five' to preserved railways, it was reported as being serviceable in early 2018.

Preserved Stanier 'Black Five' BR No 45337 is seen at Ewood Bridge on the East Lancashire Railway (ELR) on 16 April 2005 whilst topping and tailing a train with BR Standard '9F' No 92214. *Fred Kerr*

Stanier 'Black Five' BR No 45338 is seen as LMS No 5338, it was then allocated to Agecroft (26B) and is seen during a visit to Crewe during the early 1940s. *Mike Morant Collection*

This Armstrong Whitworth built locomotive (Works Number 1393) entered traffic during April 1937 as LMS No 5338 and was withdrawn from Speke Junction (8C) in October 1966. After a working life of 29 years, 5 months and 30 days it was cut up by Cashmores of Great Bridge during February 1967.

Stanier 'Black Five' BR No 45339 then allocated to Newton Heath (26A) is seen at a station location which is thought to be Bolton, during the summer of 1960 (the locomotive was allocated to 26A in during the first week of May 1960 and that allocation came to an end in August 1966). *Alan Bryant ARPS/Rail Photoprints*

This Armstrong Whitworth built locomotive (Works Number 1394) entered traffic during April 1937 as LMS No 5339 and was withdrawn from Lostock Hall (10D) in June 1967. After a working life of 30 years and 2 months it was cut up by Motherwell Machinery & Scrap of Wishaw during January 1968.

Stanier 'Black Five' BR No 45344 then allocated to Edge Hill (8A) is seen taking water on Moore troughs WCML, in 1948. *R.A. Whitfield/Rail Photoprints*

This Armstrong Whitworth built locomotive (Works Number 1399) entered traffic during April 1937 as LMS No 5344 and was withdrawn from Croes Newydd (6C) in August 1966. After a working life of 29 years and 4 months it was cut up by Cashmores of Great Bridge during March 1967.

Stanier 'Black Five' BR No 45346 then allocated to Llandudno Junction (7A) is seen approaching Frodsham station in 1948. *R.A. Whitfield/Rail Photoprints*

This Armstrong Whitworth built locomotive (Works Number 1401) entered traffic during April 1937 as LMS No 5346 and was withdrawn from Stockport Edgeley (9B) in June 1967. After a working life of 30 years and 2 months it was cut up by Cashmores of Great Bridge during November 1967.

Stanier 'Black Five' BR No 45348 then allocated to Carlisle Upperby (12B) is seen climbing to Shap Summit with a fitted freight. *Mike Morant Collection*

This Armstrong Whitworth built locomotive (Works Number 1403) entered traffic during April 1937 as LMS No 5348 and was withdrawn from Shrewsbury (6D) in August 1966. After a working life of 29 years and 4 months it was cut up by Cashmores of Great Bridge during November 1966.

Stanier 'Black Five' BR No 45351 then allocated to Carlisle Upperby (12B) is seen heading an unidentified Caprotti 'BR Standard 5' at Grange over Sands with an up-passenger service from Barrow, circa 1962. *Alan H. Bryant ARP/Rail Photoprints*

This Armstrong Whitworth built locomotive (Works Number 1406) entered traffic during May 1937 as LMS No 5351 and was withdrawn from Lostock Hall (10D) in August 1965. After a working life of 28 years, 3 months and 1 day it was sent for scrapping in January 1966 but the relevant location information is inconclusive.

Stanier 'Black Five' BR No 45360 then allocated to Inverness (60A) is seen on the turntable at Perth (63A) during July 1957. *David Anderson*

This Armstrong Whitworth built locomotive (Works Number 1415) entered traffic during May 1937 as LMS No 5360 and was withdrawn from Dalry Road (64C) in September 1965. After a working life of 28 years, 4 months and 1 day it was cut up by Motherwell Machinery & Scrap during January 1966.

Stanier 'Black Five' LMS No 5361 is seen surrounded by workers at Armstrong Whitworth, Newcastle on Tyne, on 12 May 1937, just prior to being completed. The engine is decked out in garlands, flags and a smokebox door crest to mark the occasion of the Coronation of King George VI which took place on that day. The engine's first BR allocation was to Inverness (60A). *David Anderson Collection*

This Armstrong Whitworth built locomotive (Works Number 1416) entered traffic during May 1937 as LMS No 5361 and was withdrawn from Stirling (65J) in February 1964. After a working life of 26 years, 9 months and 1 day it was cut up by Barnes & Bell of Coatbridge during June 1964.

In the 1950s and early 1960s Royalty travelled by train over the West Coast Mainline (WCML) to Edinburgh. This was for their annual summer visit to Scotland and stay at Holyrood Palace. On 3 July 1956 the Royal Train is seen passing Slateford Junction on the approaches to Edinburgh Princess Street terminus after an official visit to Lanark and Glasgow. The Royal Train on that occasion was hauled by Carlisle Kingmoor (12A) based Stanier 'Black Fives' No 45126 piloting No 45364. *David Anderson*

This Armstrong Whitworth built locomotive (Works Number 1419) entered traffic during June 1937 as LMS No 5364 and was withdrawn from Carlisle Kingmoor (12A) in August 1966. After a working life of 29 years 2 months it was cut up by Campbells of Airdrie during January 1967.

Stanier 'Black Five' BR No 45377 then allocated to Blackpool Central (24E) is seen on shed at Warrington Dallam (8B) in October 1960. *Hugh Ballantyne/Rail Photoprints*

This Armstrong Whitworth built locomotive (Works Number 1432) entered traffic during June 1937 as LMS No 5377 and was withdrawn from Bolton (9K) in December 1967. After a working life of 30 years, 5 months and 30 days it was cut up by Drapers of Hull during April 1968.

Stanier 'Black Five' BR No 45379 is seen heading a train of fitted vans in this 1963 image. *David Anderson*

This Armstrong Whitworth built locomotive (Works Number 1434) entered traffic during July 1937 as LMS No 5379 and was withdrawn from Willesden (1A) in July 1965. After a working life of 28 years, it was saved for preservation with a domed boiler, sloping throatplate, 24 element superheater and top feed on second ring of the boiler barrel.

Now preserved Stanier 'Black Five' BR No 45379 is seen in one of the many scrap lines at the yard of Woodham Brothers in Barry, South Wales during March 1966. *John Chalcraft*

Preserved Stanier 'Black Five' BR No 45379 looked to be in fine fettle when seen in 2017 on the Mid-Hants Railway (Watercress Line) at Ropley station. *Fred Kerr*

The Mid-Hants Railway Preservation Society (MHRPS) owns and operates BR No 45379. In 1974 the locomotive was bought for restoration and initially taken to the Avon Valley Railway, it later moved to The Great Central Railway. It was purchased from there by MHRPS and arrived at Alresford, Hampshire in March 2002.

When newly restored the 'Black Five' took part in the railways Somerset & Dorset Steam Spectacular on 10–12 September 2010. The restoration effort took five years to complete. BR No 45379 had not steamed since 1965, so the aforementioned S&D event was the first time the locomotive had hauled a revenue earning service for over 45 years. The engine is now regularly rostered to haul trains and more information can be found on the railways web-site at www.watercressline.co.uk

A trio of work stained Stanier locomotives seen in light steam outside Rose Grove shed (10F) on 28 March 1968. Left to right: '8F' BR No 48666, '8F' BR No 48730 and 'Black Five' BR No 45382. Note lack of shed code plates, replaced by painted numbers. *Hugh Ballantyne/Rail Photoprints*

This Armstrong Whitworth built locomotive (Works Number 1437) entered traffic during July 1937 as LMS No 5382 and was withdrawn from Rose Grove (10F) in June 1968. After a working life of 30 years, 11 months and 1 day it was cut up by Drapers of Hull during December 1968.

Stanier 'Black Five' LMS No 5390 (BR 45390) is seen on Camden Bank during 1939. First BR allocation for this locomotive was Aston (3D). *Dave Cobb Collection/ Rail Photoprints*

This Armstrong Whitworth built locomotive (Works Number 1445) entered traffic during August 1937 as LMS No 5390 and was withdrawn from Carnforth (10A) in August 1968. After a working life of 31 years it was cut up by Drapers of Hull during October 1968.

Stanier 'Black Five' LMS No 5390 (BR 45390) is seen next to Euston station No 1 Signal Box during October 1937. Note also the Horwich 1931 built 'Jinty' LMS No 7669 (BR 47669) which was probably on station pilot duty. *Mike Morant Collection*

Stanier 'Black Five' BR No 45391 then allocated to Crewe South (5B) is seen on Moore troughs and it looks from the tender tank overflow to be overdoing the filling process as it heads north with train 1Z78, during June 1965. *Colin Whitfield/Rail Photoprints*

This Armstrong Whitworth built locomotive (Works Number 1446) entered traffic during August 1937 as LMS No 5391 and was withdrawn from Lostock Hall (10D) in February 1968. After a working life of 30 years and 6 months it was cut up by T.W. Ward of Sheffield during June 1968.

Stanier 'Black Five' BR No 45403 seen on the turntable at the locomotive's then home shed of Shrewsbury (6D), during 1965. Note the other locomotives which include a Franco Crosti BR 9F which by that date had its boiler converted back to conventional operation (with the pre-heat bottom section blanked off) thereby reclassifying it to 8F. *Rail Photoprints Collection*

This Armstrong Whitworth built locomotive (Works Number 1458) entered traffic during August 1937 as LMS No 5403 and was withdrawn from Chester (6A) in September 1966. After a working life of 29 years and 1 month it was cut up by Cashmores of Great Bridge during January 1967.

Stanier 'Black Five' BR No 45407 then allocated to Nottingham (16A) is seen climbing up to Chinley North Junction with the up 'Palatine', circa 1959. 'The Palatine' London St. Pancras–Manchester Central, first titled run on 4 July 1938. The title was withdrawn on 9 September 1939 and re-introduced on 16 September 1957 with the final titled run taking place on 13 June 1964. *Alan H. Bryant/Rail Photoprints*

This Armstrong Whitworth built locomotive (Works Number 1462) entered traffic during September 1937 as LMS No 5407 and was withdrawn from Lostock Hall (10D) in August 1968. After a working life of 30 years and 11 months it was saved for preservation with a domed boiler, sloping throatplate, 24 element superheater and top feed on the second ring of the boiler barrel.

Preserved Stanier 'Black Five' LMS No 5407 is seen on the Settle & Carlisle route with a Cumbrian Mountain Express service in 1984. *Keith Langston Collection*

One of the final Stanier 'Black Five' locomotives in operation, BR No 45407 was withdrawn on 4 August 1968. Dr. Peter Beet, the co-founder of Steamtown Carnforth, with Sir Bill McAlpine and business partner David Davis visited Lostock Hall depot to choose a locomotive to save, and No 45407 was selected. It initially became part of the Steamtown collection, where for some time it was painted in Furness Railway Indian red livery.

In 1974, it was bought by Paddy Smith, who immediately returned it to LMS livery. He operated the engine on various enthusiast tours, including the Settle-Carlisle Line, the Cambrian Coast Express, the Crewe to Holyhead Line; and The Jacobite between Fort William and Mallaig, where it spent three seasons in the late 1980s. After the last season in Scotland, No 45407 was returned to Carnforth, and then moved to the East Lancashire Railway to work out the last three years of its boiler certificate.

In 1997, Ian Riley bought the engine, and it was subsequently overhauled at the works of Riley and Son, Bury. That work included the fabrication of a new tender with increased water capacity, the installation of air brake equipment to enable the engine to haul modern coaching stock and the fitting of A.W.S. to comply modern mainline safety and signalling requirements.

In 2010, No 45407 underwent another overhaul, which is believed to be the fastest ever undertaken on a mainline locomotive in preservation, reportedly completed in only 14 weeks. In 2017 the locomotives home base was stated as being the East Lancashire Railway (ELR) at Bury.

In preservation BR No 45407 has carried the name THE LANCASHIRE FUSILIER.

Preserved Stanier 'Black Five' BR No 45407, then carrying a Bury (26D) shed plate is seen alongside the Conway estuary at Glan Conway station, whilst heading up to Blaenau Ffestiniog on 1 May 1999. Note the Welsh Dragon style headboard. *Keith Langston Collection*

When first preserved Stanier 'Black Five' LMS No 5407 is seen at Steamtown painted in a re-creation of the former Furness Railway 'Indian red' livery. *Mike Morant Collection*

Stanier 'Black Five' BR No 45422 then carrying a Shrewsbury (84G) shed plate approaches Builth Road High Level with the 7.45am Swansea Victoria – Shrewsbury service, on 7 June 1960. Note all the trackside workers and not a hi-vis jacket in sight! *Hugh Ballantyne/Rail Photoprints*

This Armstrong Whitworth built locomotive (Works Number 1477) entered traffic during October 1937 as LMS No 5422 and was withdrawn from Stoke (5D) in September 1966. After a working life of 28 years, 11 months and 1 day it was cut up by Cashmores of Great Bridge during December 1966.

Stanier 'Black Five' BR No 45423 then allocated to Stirling (63B) is seen passing Robroyston with a seven-coach stopping passenger train 23 February 1961. *J & J Collection – Sid Rickard/Rail Photoprints*

This Armstrong Whitworth built locomotive (Works Number 1478) entered traffic during October 1937 as LMS No 5423 and was withdrawn from Motherwell (66B) in May 1967. After a working life of 29 years and 7 months it was cut up by J. McWilliams of Shettleston during September 1967.

This Armstrong Whitworth built locomotive (Works Number 1483) entered traffic during October 1937 as LMS No 5428 and was withdrawn from Leeds Holbeck (55A) in October 1967. After a working life of 30 years it was saved for preservation with a domed boiler, sloping throatplate, 24 element superheater and top feed on second boiler barrel ring.

Preserved BR No 45428 was a Leeds Holbeck (20A) 1948 to 1957 thereafter (55A) allocated locomotive on two occasions 3/12/1955 to 7/04/59 and 8/10/1996 until being withdrawn. In addition to working main line trains, Holbeck 'Class Fives' regularly worked summer specials from the West Riding to Whitby, via York, Malton, Pickering and what is now the North Yorkshire Moors Railway (NYMR); thus 'Black Fives' became a familiar sight through Newtondale, and it is thought that BR No 45428 was one of them.

The locomotive hauled the last steam worked London bound express from Bradford to Leeds on I October 1967 and was withdrawn a week later when steam traction was abandoned in the Leeds area, and indeed throughout the North-East region of BR.

Preserved at the NYMR in 1967 the locomotive was named ERIC TREACY after the former Bishop of Wakefield, an eminent railway photographer.

At the time of writing the locomotive was undergoing a 7-year boiler repair and was reportedly expected back in service during 2018.

Preserved Stanier 'Black Five' BR 45428 ERIC TREACY is seen departing Whitby on the NYMR, August 2010. *NYMR*

https://www.youtube.com/watch?v=8vZIIPR_cNY
*Firing and driving Black Five BR No 45428 between Grosmont and Pickering* – NYMR Footage

Preserved Stanier 'Black Five', seen as LMS No 5428 leaves a smoke trail as it crosses the spectacular Glenfinnan Viaduct with the 10.55 Fort William – Mallaig steam service, circa 1987. *Colin Whitfield/Rail Photoprints*

# 1938

**45452–45471 September–December, 20 locomotives built at Crewe Works**
Introduced with Domed Boilers, Sloping Throatplates and 28 element Superheaters, locomotive wheelbase 27ft 2in.

Stanier 'Black Five' BR No 45452 is nicely framed by an overbridge as it backs down to Perth station (visible in the distance) from the shed in preparation for a southbound working, circa 1959. *David Anderson*

This Crewe Works built locomotive (Lot 142) entered traffic during September 1938 as LMS No 5452 and was withdrawn from Carstairs (66E) in June 1963. After a working life of 24 years, 3 months and 28 days (allocated only to Scottish sheds) it was cut up by Motherwell Machinery & Scrap of Wishaw during September 1963.

Ex LMS Horwich 'Crab' BR No 42800 and Stanier 'Black Five' BR No 45460 both locomotives were at that time allocated to Ayr Shed (67C). They are seen double heading a Stranraer-Glasgow passenger train at Girvan Station, as No 42800 is taking water on 13 July 1963. *J & J Collection – Sid Rickard/Rail Photoprints*

This Crewe Works built locomotive (Lot 142) entered traffic during October 1938 as LMS No 5460 and was withdrawn from Ayr in June 1965. After a working life of 26 years, 8 months and 1 day (allocated only to Scottish sheds) it was cut up by Arnott Young of Troon during June 1968.

Stanier 'Black Five' BR No 45461 is seen passing Garngaber Junction, to the east of Lenzie, with an eastbound 'Class J' freight on 10 February 1962. *J & J Collection – Sid Rickard/Rail Photoprints*

This Crewe Works built locomotive (Lot 142) entered traffic during October 1938 as LMS No 5461 and was withdrawn from Perth (63A) in June 1965. After a working life of 27 years, 10 months and 1 day (allocated only to Scottish sheds) it was cut up by Motherwell Machinery & Scrap of Wishaw during November 1966.

Stanier 'Black Five' BR No 45461 then allocated to Perth Shed (63A) and seen in clean condition is waiting for the road from Robroyston Yard with a train consisting of two ex-works carriages and a brake van on 23 February 1961. *J & J Collection – Sid Rickard/Rail Photoprints*

Stanier 'Black Five' BR No 45463 then allocated to Ardrossan (67D) is seen whilst waiting to depart from Glasgow St. Enoch station on 24 July 1961. *Rail Photoprints Collection*

This Crewe Works built locomotive (Lot 142) entered traffic during November 1938 as LMS No 5463 and was withdrawn from Stranraer (67F) in November 1966. After a working life of 28 years (allocated only to Scottish sheds) it was cut up by Motherwell Machinery & Scrap of Wishaw during April 1967.

Stanier 'Black Five' BR No 45466 then allocated to Carlisle Kingmoor (68A) is seen whilst departing Elvanfoot with the 12.40pm to Carlisle on 16 April 1955. *David Anderson*

This Crewe Works built locomotive (Lot 142) entered traffic during November 1938 as LMS No 5466 and was withdrawn from Speke Junction (8C) in February 1967. After a working life of 28 years and 3 months it was cut up by Cashmores of Great Bridge during May 1967.

Stanier 'Black Five' BR No 45467 then allocated to Glasgow Corkerhill (67A) is seen in the rock cutting near Cowlairs Junction with a westbound freight during January 1961.
*J & J Collection – Sid Rickard/Rail Photoprints*

This Crewe Works built locomotive (Lot 142) entered traffic during November 1938 as LMS No 5467 and was withdrawn from Motherwell (66B) in December 1966. After a working life of 28 years and 30 days (allocated only to Scottish sheds) it was cut up by J. McWilliams of Shettleston during April 1967.

Stanier 'Black Five' BR No 45468 which was allocated to St. Rollox (65B) for all of its BR working life, departs Strathyre with the 7.50am Glasgow to Oban. 'Black Five' BR No 45359 (a 1937 Armstrong Whitworth built locomotive withdrawn May 1967) is waiting in the loop line and would follow northbound with the Stirling to Oban daily freight on 24 August 1960. *Hugh Ballantyne/Rail Photoprints*

This Crewe Works built locomotive (Lot 142) entered traffic during December 1938 as LMS No 5468 and was withdrawn from St. Rollox (66B) in May 1964. After a working life of 25 years and 5 months it was cut up by Connels of Coatbridge during November 1964.

# 1943

## 45472-45491 April-December, 20 locomotives built at Derby Works

ntroduced with Domed Boilers, Sloping Throatplates and 28 element Superheaters, locomotive wheelbase 27ft 2in. All boilers constructed at Crewe Works. Following GWR practice Stanier specified tapered flat rectangular-section coupling rods but retained I-section for the connecting rods.

From 1943 onwards, I-section material was used for both connecting and coupling rods as can be clearly seen from the relevant images.

Stanier 'Black Five' BR No 45477 then allocated to St. Margarets (64A) is seen being headed by BRC&W 'Type 2' No D5366 with a Stranraer – Ayr van train, proceeding north over Pinmore Viaduct on 19 March 1966. *Derek Cross/ Rail Photoprints*

This Derby Works built locomotive (Lot 151) entered traffic during July 1943 as LMS No 5477 and was withdrawn from St. Margarets in August 1966. After a working life of 23 years, 1 month and 1 day (allocated only to Scottish sheds) it was cut up by Motherwell Machinery & Scrap of Wishaw during January 1967.

In this busy Scottish Region image Stanier 'Black Five' BR No 45482 then allocated to Grangemouth (65F) is seen piloted by Horwich 'Crab' BR No 42803 at the platform of Girvan Station with a Glasgow – Stranraer boat train, the I section rods can clearly be seen. An unidentified 'Crab' heading another 'Black Five' is seen approaching with a Stranraer–Glasgow boat train on 13 July 1963. Note the DMU in the holding siding to the right. *J & J Collection – Sid Rickard/Rail Photoprints*

This Derby Works built locomotive (Lot 152) entered traffic during September 1943 as LMS No 5482 and was withdrawn from Grangemouth in June 1964. After a working life of 20 years and 9 months it was cut up by Motherwell Machinery & Scrap of Wishaw during November 1964.

Stanier 'Black Five' BR No 45485 then allocated to Motherwell (66B) is seen climbing Beattock Bank with a train of steel flats, circa 1959. This domed boiler example has the top feed located on the second boiler ring in front of the dome. The driver is making sure that the photographer captures him in the image. *David Anderson*

This Derby Works built locomotive (Lot 152) entered traffic during October 1943 as LMS No 5485 and was withdrawn from Stranraer (68C) in October 1963. After a working life of 20 years (allocated only to Scottish sheds) it was cut up by Barnes & Bell of Coatbridge during July 1964.

Stanier 'Black Five' BR No 45487 then allocated to Grangemouth (65F) is seen tender first near Fouldubbs Junction, with a 'Class K' rake of mineral empties from Grangemouth. Note the timber yard to the right of the engine which has its own private sidings, 30 June 1963. *J & J Collection – Sid Rickard/Rail Photoprints*

This Derby Works built locomotive (Lot 152) entered traffic during November 1943 as LMS No 5487 and was withdrawn from Grangemouth in February 1964. After a working life of 20 years and 3 months it was cut up by Connels of Coatbridge during November 1964.

Stanier 'Black Five' BR No 45490 is seen stored out of use at Polmadie (66A) Glasgow, 26 March 1967. Note that the shed plate and number plate have been removed. This domed boiler example has the top feed located on the front ring of the boiler barrel with the feed pipe under the cladding. *Rail Photoprints*

This Derby Works built locomotive (Lot 152) entered traffic during December 1943 as LMS No 5490 and was withdrawn from Motherwell (66B) in December 1966. After a working life of 23 years (allocated only to Scottish sheds) it was cut up by J. McWilliams of Shettleston during June 1967.

Later to be preserved Stanier 'Black Five' BR No 45491, then allocated to Carlisle Kingmoor (12A) waits at Heads of Ayr station (for Butlins Holiday Camp) with the 08.35 (So) service to Leeds, 24 June 1961. The station, opened to serve the holiday camp closed on 16 September 1963. *J & J Collection – Sid Rickard/Rail Photoprints*

This Derby Works built locomotive (Lot 152) entered traffic during December 1943 as LMS No 5491 and was withdrawn from Carlisle Kingmoor in July 1965. After a working life of 21 years and 7 months it was saved for preservation. For more information visit http://www.gcrailway. co.uk/the-railway/locomotives/45491-2/

Stanier 'Black Five' BR No 45491-boiler work in progress June 2015. *Phil Brown*

After being withdrawn BR No 45491 was sold for scrap and moved to Woodham Brothers at Barry, South Wales in October 1965. It languished there for almost 16 years before being bought and rescued by the 'West Lancashire Black 5 Society' and moved to the ICI works at Hillhouse in 1981. The locomotive was subsequently moved to the Fleetwood Steam Centre before being purchased by its current owner Phil Wainwright and moved to the Midland Railway Centre at Butterly, in September 1991. As withdrawn, the Derby built locomotive is the only surviving example to have a boiler with top feed on the front ring in conjunction with Walschaerts valve gear. It then moved to the Great Central Railway (GCR) at Quorn & Woodhouse in 2011.

Stanier 'Black Five' BR No 45491-rolling chassis and cylinders work in progress, June 2015. *Phil Brown*

In September 2017, the Loughborough Standard Locomotives Group Ltd reported the locomotive's restoration was progressing well with work to the chassis and tender almost complete. Other work has included replacing 3 of the bogie axleboxes (the originals were reportedly stolen) new tyres being fitted to the driving wheels, re-boring the cylinders, and locating and/or manufacturing numerous missing components. The boiler is a work in progress and has included the installation of a new firebox tube plate, together with a copper internal steam pipe.

The boiler and firebox of preserved Stanier 'Black Five' BR No 45491 is seen again in September 2017 as work progresses towards a hydraulic and steam test. Note also the smokebox and boiler of preserved Stanier 'Black Five' BR No 45305 (a 1937 Armstrong Whitworth built example) and regular visitor to the GCR which was at that time receiving attention. *Phil Brown*

# 1944

## 45492–45499 January–April, 8 locomotives built at Derby Works

Introduced with Domed Boilers, Sloping Throatplates and 28 element Superheaters, locomotive wheelbase 27ft 2in. All boilers constructed at Crewe Works. On 1 January 1946 locomotive BR No 45495 from this batch was involved in an accident at Lichfield Trent Valley station.

After derailing with a freight train, due to faulty points a fatal collision with a passenger train then occurred. The locomotive was returned to service after repair.

Stanier 'Black Five' BR No 45493 then allocated to Banbury (2D) substituted for the booked engine 'V2' 2-6-2 BR No 60919 which had failed. The Locomotive Club of Great Britain (LCGB') 'Green Arrow' Railtour of 3 July 1966 is seen at Weymouth with the 'Black Five' heading Bulleid Pacific BR No 34100 APPLEDORE, sadly the booked engine (60919) failed and 45493 substituted; it is seen partnering 34100 'Appledore' as the train arrives at Weymouth. *John Chalcraft/Rail Photoprints*

This Derby Works built locomotive (Lot 153) entered traffic during January 1944 as LMS No 5493 and was withdrawn from Carlisle Kingmoor (12A) in January 1968. After a working life of 24 years it was cut up by Drapers of Hull during April 1968.

Stanier 'Black Five' BR No 45497 then allocated to Perth (63A) is seen at Kyle of Lochalsh station with a mixed train comprising parcel vans, postal coach and passenger vehicles. Note the 'wheel tapper' inspecting the train and also the single line tablet equipment mounted on the cab side, circa 1960. The station at Kyle of Lochalsh occupied one of the most picturesque settings in Britain with the magnificent Isle of Skye as its backdrop. *David Anderson*

This Derby Works built locomotive (Lot 153) entered traffic during April 1944 as LMS No 5497 and was withdrawn from Ayr (67C) during February 1964. After a working life of 19 years and 10 months it was cut up by Connels of Coatbridge during October 1964.

## 44800-44825 May-December, 26 locomotives built at Derby Works

Introduced with Domed Boilers, Sloping Throatplates and 28 element Superheaters, locomotive wheelbase 27ft 2in. Boilers constructed at Crewe Works.

Stanier 'Black Five' BR No 44801 then allocated to Perth (63A) is seen hard at work on Beattock Bank, circa 1959.
*David Anderson*

Preserved Stanier 'Black Five' BR No 44806 is seen at Carrog Station on the Llangollen Railway whilst masquerading as sister engine BR No 44801, complete with blue backed front number plate and shed plate.
*Keith Langston Collection*

This Derby Works built locomotive (Lot 153) entered traffic during May 1944 as LMS No 4801 and was withdrawn from Hurlford (67B) during May 1964. After a working life of 20 years it was cut up by Cowlairs Works during September 1964.

BR No 44806 was an early candidate for preservation, moving directly from BR to the "Steamtown" collection at Carnforth. It had fortunately avoided the usual years of neglect and parts-stripping at Woodham Brothers scrapyard in Barry, Vale of Glamorgan, South Wales. It was unusually well-travelled between museums and lines. In 1973, after some years spent based in Accrington the locomotive was based for a short time at the then newly reopened Lakeside and Haverthwaite Railway. Whilst there, it was named MAGPIE after the children's TV series. In 1983, whilst side-lined with boiler/firebox problems, MAGPIE moved to Manchester and the Museum of Science and Industry, as a static exhibit. In 1993 the locomotive was moved again this time to Llangollen where after a three-year repair programme it steamed again and worked regularly for almost ten years, in both LMS and BR liveries. Since its initial preservation, BR No 44806 had been privately owned by one man, Ken Aldcroft. Mr Aldcroft died in 2003, and the ownership of the locomotive passed to his family. To commemorate those 35 years of preservation, the 'Black Five' was renamed KENNETH ALDCROFT.

In July 2013, the locomotive was offered for sale, and subsequently purchased by the North Yorkshire Moors Railway. For more information visit the NYMR web-site at https://www.nymr.co.uk/

Preserved Stanier 'Black Five' BR No 44806 as LMS 4806 is seen with a dining train at Glyndyfrdwy on the Llangollen Railway during August 2007. At that time the locomotive carried the preservation era name MAGPIE. *Keith Langston Collection*

This Derby Works built locomotive (Lot 153) entered traffic during July 1944 as LMS No 4806 and was withdrawn from Lostock Hall (10D) during August 1968. After a working life of 24 years, 1 month and 1 day it was saved for preservation with a domed sloping throatplate boiler, 24 element superheater and top feed on the second ring of the boiler barrel.

Preserved Stanier 'Black Five' BR No 44806 MAGPIE then carrying a Speke Junction (8C) shed plate is seen at Glyndyfrdwy on the Llangollen Railway in 1998. Note that the headboard commemorates the fact that ex-Chairman and Llangollen Railway stalwart had been awarded an MBE for his services to railway preservation. *Keith Langston Collection*

Preserved Stanier 'Black Five' BR No 44806 is seen masquerading as Scottish allocated sister engine BR No 44801 during an April 2009 Steel, Steam & Stars event, whilst approaching Garth-y- Dwr. The headboard commemorates the '1962 RCTS/SLS Scottish Rail Tour'. *Keith Langston Collection*

Stanier 'Black Five' BR No 44807 then allocated to Holyhead (6J) is seen passing the now out of use, but listed building Rhyl No 2-signal box whilst arriving with the 10.30 Llandudno–Manchester Exchange, on 7 August 1965. *Ian Turnbull/Rail Photoprints Collection*

This Derby Works built locomotive (Lot 170) entered traffic during September 1944 as LMS No 4807 and was withdrawn from Trafford Park (9E) during March 1968. After a working life of 23 years, 5 months and 29 days it was cut up by Drapers of Hull during June 1968.

Stanier 'Black Five' BR No 44808 then allocated to Patricroft (26F) is seen approaching Chester General station with a North Wales bound service, circa 1962. Note that the sighting of the locomotive is being recorded by the two young gentlemen on the adjacent platform. *Alan H. Bryant ARPS/Rail Photoprints Collection*

This Derby Works built locomotive (Lot 170) entered traffic during September 1944 as LMS No 4808 and was withdrawn from Oxley (2B) during April 1965. After a working life of 22 years, 2 months and 30 days it was cut up by Drapers of Hull during December 1967.

Stanier 'Black Five' locomotives. BR No 44811 then allocated to Leicester Midland (15C) is seen at Dalry Road, Edinburgh in the company of BR No 45434 then allocated to Crewe North (5A) and built Armstrong Whitworth in 1937. In the summer timetable during the mid-1950s and early 1960s, a through direct express passenger service was scheduled to run from Birmingham New Street to Edinburgh Princes Street. On this occasion the service was double headed by these two locomotives and here they are being hand coaled in preparation for the return journey on the following day. *David Anderson*

This Derby Works built locomotive (Lot 170) entered traffic during October 1944 as LMS No 4811 and was withdrawn from Colwick (16B) during October 1966. After a working life of 22 years it was cut up by Drapers of Hull during February 1967.

Stanier 'Black Five' BR No 44817 then allocated to Kentish Town (14B) is seen on shed at Neasden (14D) during June 1960. *Ian Turnbull/Rail Photoprints Collection*

This Derby Works built locomotive (Lot 170) entered traffic during November 1944 as LMS No 4817 and was withdrawn from Carlisle Kingmoor (12A) during August 1967. After a working life of 22 years and 9 months it was cut up by J. McWilliams of Shettleston during December 1967.

Stanier 'Black Five' BR No 44820 then allocated to Motherwell (66B) passes Saltcoats with a Motherwell–Largs excursion, 15 June 1963. Note the coal mine and waste tips on the right of the skyline. *J & J Collection – Sid Rickard/Rail Photoprints*

This Derby Works built locomotive (Lot 170) entered traffic during December 1944 as LMS No 4820 and was withdrawn from Motherwell during December 1966. After a working life of 22 years it was cut up by J. McWilliams of Shettleston during December 1967.

Stanier 'Black Five' BR No 44821 then allocated to Kentish Town (14B) passes Gowhole on the approach to New Mills South Junction with a down express for Manchester, during August 1961. *Alan H. Bryant ARPS/Rail Photoprints*

This Derby Works built locomotive (Lot 170) entered traffic during December 1944 as LMS No 4821 and was withdrawn from Crewe South (5B) during June 1967. After a working life of 22 years, 6 months and 1 day it was cut up by Cohens of Kettering during December 1967.

Stanier 'Black Five' BR No 44825 at that time allocated to Colwick (40E) is seen with the 'Railway Enthusiasts Club' 'The Collier' brake van tour IT05 around coal pits in the Nottingham area, this stop over is at Gedling Colliery 9 July 1966. *Rail Photoprints Collection*

This Derby Works built locomotive (Lot 170) entered traffic during December 1944 as LMS No 4825 and was withdrawn from Carlisle Kingmoor (12A) during October 1967. After a working life of 22 years and 10 months it was cut up by J. McWilliams of Shettleston during February 1968.

## 44826–44860 July–December, 35 locomotives built at Crewe Works
Introduced with Domed Boilers, Sloping Throatplates and 28 element Superheaters, locomotive wheelbase 27ft 2in.

Stanier 'Black Five' BR No 44827 then allocated to Llandudno Junction (6G) hauls a train of imported Irish Beef cattle (ex-Holyhead Docks) heading for English abattoirs. The train is seen passing along the North Wales coast at Penmaenmawr on 9 August 1960. This view was taken before the A55 by-pass to the area was built. *Derek Cross/Rail Photoprints*

This Crewe Works built locomotive (Lot 170) entered traffic during July 1944 as LMS No 4827 and was withdrawn from Edge Hill (8A) during July 1965. After a working life of 22 years it was cut up by Cashmores of Great Bridge during December 1965.

Stanier 'Black Five' BR No 44828 then allocated to Holbeck (20A) calls at Skipton with the 10.35 Morecambe–Bradford (Forster Square) service, 22 July 1967, only two months before the locomotive was withdrawn. Note the different liveries of the coaching stock. *Ian Turnbull/Rail Photoprints Collection*

This Crewe Works built locomotive (Lot 170) entered traffic during July 1944 as LMS No 4828 and was withdrawn from Holbeck (20A) during September 1967. After a working life of 23 years, 2 months and 1 day it was cut up by Cashmores of Great Bridge during September 1967.

Stanier 'Black Five' BR
No 44829 then allocated
to Saltley (2E) is seen on
the East Curve heading to
Didcot North Junction in
the company of Stanier
'8F' BR No 48006 on 27
September 1964.
*David Anderson*

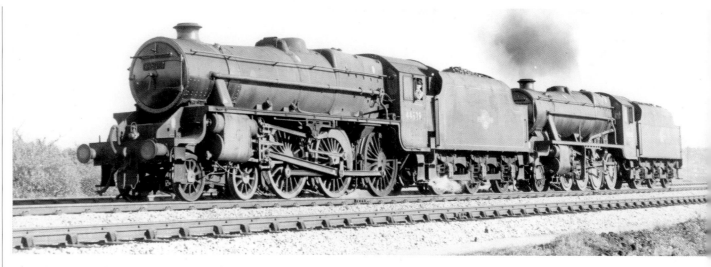

This Crewe Works built locomotive (Lot 170) entered traffic during August 1944 as LMS No 4829 and was withdrawn from Bolton (9K) during May 1968. After a working life of 23 years, 8 months and 30 days it was cut up during August 1968 (location uncertain).

Stanier 'Black Five' BR
No 44832 then allocated
to Crewe North (5A) is
seen with a down train
of fitted vans at Winwick
Junction during March
1963. *Rail Photoprints
Collection*

This Crewe Works built locomotive (Lot 170) entered traffic during August 1944 as LMS No 4832 and was withdrawn from Crewe North (5A) during September 1967. After a working life of 23 years and 1 month it was cut up by T.W. Ward of Killamarsh during December 1967.

Stanier 'Black Five' BR No 44836 then allocated to Rugby (1F) is seen at Crewe Works during 1965. *Brian Robbins/Rail Photoprints*

This Crewe Works built locomotive (Lot 170) entered traffic during September 1944 as LMS No 4836 and was withdrawn from Stockport Edgeley (9B) during May 1968. After a working life of 23 years, 7 months and 30 days it was cut up by T.W. Ward of Sheffield during September 1968.

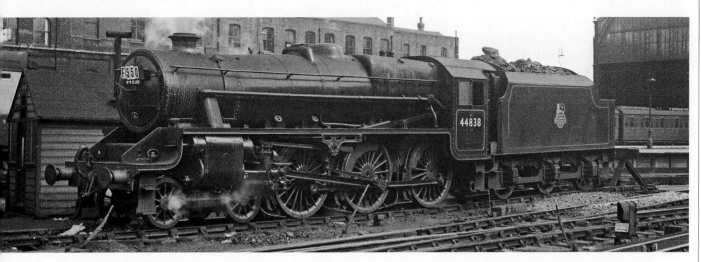

Stanier 'Black Five' BR No 44838 then allocated to Willesden (1A) is seen at Brighton during 1956. *Rail Photo Prints Collection*

This Crewe Works built locomotive (Lot 170) entered traffic during September 1944 as LMS No 4838 and was withdrawn from Edge Hill (8A) during March 1968. After a working life of 23 years, 5 months and 29 days it was cut up by Cohens of Kettering during June 1968.

Stanier 'Black Five' with early BR No 4840M a system of numbering used on some locomotives during the 1948 transitional period with the M denoting London Midland Region (did not receive its full BR number until 1950). The locomotive is seen at Willesden (1A) in 1948, shortly after receiving British Railways livery. *Rail Photoprints Collection*

This Crewe Works built locomotive (Lot 170) entered traffic during October 1944 as LMS No 4840 and was withdrawn from Birkenhead (8H) during November 1967. After a working life of 23 years, 1 months and 1 day it was cut up by Cashmores of Great Bridge during February 1968.

Stanier 'Black Five' No 44841 then allocated to Saltley (21A) is seen whilst working hard with a lengthy mixed freight in an un-identified location, circa 1960. *Rail Photoprints Collection*

This Crewe Works built locomotive (Lot 170) entered traffic during October 1944 as LMS No 4841 and was withdrawn from Oxley (2B) during October 1966. After a working life of 22 years it was cut up by Cashmores of Great Bridge during February 1968.

Stanier 'Black Five' BR No 44847 then allocated to Annesley (16B) is seen at London Marylebone station on 19 September 1964 after arriving with the 8.15am service from Nottingham Victoria. This splendid period image shows a poster for the film Cleopatra starring Elizabeth Taylor and Richard Burton, then showing at the Dominion picture house. Note also the boxes of Farley's Teething Rusks and the wooden packing station egg crates, loaded onto a truck between platform edges. At this busy commuter station that adds a whole new meaning to the phrase, go to work on an egg! *Hugh Ballantyne/Rail Photoprints*

This Crewe Works built locomotive (Lot 170) entered traffic during November 1944 as LMS No 4847 and was withdrawn from Colwick (16B) during November 1966. After a working life of 22 years it was cut up by Cashmores of Great Bridge during May 1967.

Stanier 'Black Five' BR No 44853 spent all of its working life at Leeds Holbeck (20A and later 55A), here it is seen in a clean condition passing Slutchers Lane Signal box, Warrington with a coal working, circa 1963. Note the circle with inverted triangle HALT road sign to the front right of the locomotive. *Colin Whitfield/ Rail Photoprints*

This Crewe Works built locomotive (Lot 170) entered traffic during November 1944 as LMS No 4853 and was withdrawn from Holbeck during June 1967. After a working life of 22 years and 7 months it was cut up by Cohens of Kettering during November 1967.

Stanier 'Black Five' BR No 44855 then allocated to Bristol Barrow Road (22A) is seen in BR livery during a visit to Crewe Works during the summer of 1950. Note the trilby wearing 'boss' leaning on the lever of the ground frame! *Rail Photoprints Collection*

This Crewe Works built locomotive (Lot 170) entered traffic during December 1944 as LMS No 4855 and was withdrawn from Stockport Edgeley (9B) during May 1968. After a working life of 23 years and 5 months it was cut up by T.W. Ward of Sheffield during September 1968.

Stanier 'Black Five' BR No 44858 then allocated to Colwick (16B) is seen near Chorley Wood with the 2.30 Marylebone-Nottingham, 17 August 1966, when in need of a good clean.
*Dave Cobbe/Rail Photoprints Collection*

This Crewe Works built locomotive (Lot 170) entered traffic during December 1944 as LMS No 4858 and was withdrawn from Carlisle Kingmoor (12A) during December 1967. After a working life of 23 years it was cut up by T.W. Ward of Killamarsh during March 1968.

Stanier 'Black Five' BR No 44859 then allocated to Saltley (2E) seen in what the photographer's notes rightly described as 'deplorable external condition' draws a northbound freight out of Basford Hall down yard and onto the down Independent Lines bypassing Crewe station in falling snow, on 4 February 1965. *Colin Whitfield/Rail Photoprints*

This Crewe Works built locomotive (Lot 170) entered traffic during December 1944 as LMS No 4859 and was withdrawn from Birkenhead (8H) during November 1967. After a working life of 22 years, 11 months and 1 day it was cut up by Cashmores of Great Bridge during March 1968.

# 1945

## 44861–44920 January–December, 60 locomotives built at Crewe Works
Introduced with Domed Boilers, Sloping Throatplates and 28 element Superheaters, locomotive wheelbase 27ft 2in.

Stanier 'Black Five' BR No 44864 then allocated to Llandudno Junction (6G) heads west near Dunham Hill (between Frodsham and Helsby) with the Manchester–Llandudno evening commuter service, during April 1959. *R. A. Whitfield/ Rail Photoprints*

This Crewe Works built locomotive (Lot 170) entered traffic during January 1945 as LMS No 4864 and was withdrawn from Edge Hill (8A) in May 1968. After a working life of 23 years, 3 months and 30 days it was cut up by T.W. Ward of Killamarsh during July 1968.

Stanier 'Black Five' BR No 44869 then allocated to Northampton (2E) heads north over Moore troughs with a down excursion, during August 1963. *R. A. Whitfield/Rail Photoprints*

This Crewe Works built locomotive (Lot 170) entered traffic during March 1945 as LMS No 4869 and was withdrawn from Heaton Mersey (9F) in September 1966. After a working life of 21 years, 6 months and 3 days it was cut up by Drapers of Hull during February 1967.

Stanier 'Black Five' locomotives BR No 44871 then allocated to Carnforth (11A) and later preserved and BR No 44894 then also allocated to Carnforth (11A) prepare to leave Manchester Victoria with the SLS 'Farewell to Steam No 1' train 'A' railtour, on 4 August 1968. The train originated and terminated at Birmingham New Street and the non-steam sections were electric and diesel locomotive hauled by E3093 and D7588 respectively. Steam route Manchester Victoria-Diggle-Huddersfield-Sowerby Bridge-Copy Pit-Blackburn – (via Bolton avoiding line) – Wigan Wallgate-Kirkby-Bootle-Stanley-Rainhill-Barton Moss-Manchester Victoria-Droylesden-Stockport. *Colin Whitfield/Rail Photoprints*

This Crewe Works built locomotive (Lot 170) entered traffic during March 1945 as LMS No 4871 and was withdrawn from Carnforth in August 1968. After a working life of 23 years, 5 months and 3 days it was saved for preservation with a sloping throat plate domed boiler, 24 element superheater and top feed on second ring of boiler barrel.

Stanier 'Black Five' BR No 44871 was purchased directly from British Railways for preservation and so never had to be restored from scrapyard condition, unlike many other preserved locomotives. The locomotive survived until the end of BR steam (August 1968) and was accordingly one of four locomotives chosen to take part in the famous 'Fifteen Guinea Special' on 11 August 1968.

The 'Fifteen Guinea Special' used four steam locomotives BR No 45110, BR No 70013 OLIVER CROMWELL and 'Black Five' locomotives BR No 44781 and BR No 44871, which worked double headed for the return Carlisle – Manchester Victoria leg. No 44871 has frequently been seen on the national network and additionally visited various heritage railways. Because of regular maintenance and various rebuilds this 'Black Five' has up to date spent over 50 years in preservation with many of those in steam. Its preservation life is well over double the period which it worked for the LMS and BR. Currently owned by Riley & Son of Bury, the locomotive has been kept in mainline running order with its present boiler certificate set to expire in 2024.

'Black Five' BR No 44871 at Stockport Edgeley in 1962. *Hugh Ballantyne/Rail Photoprints*

'Black Five' BR No 44871 and 'Britannia' 70013 OLIVER CROMWELL pass Barton Hill, Bristol with Bristol–Preston 'Great Briton III', on 8 April 2010. *John Chalcraft/ Rail Photoprints*

Preserved Stanier 'Black Five' BR No 44871 is seen in this dramatic image near Corrour whilst crossing Rannoch Moor on 16 October 2010. The Great Moor of Rannoch is one of the last remaining wildernesses in Europe and is a beautiful outdoor space stretching far north and west from Rannoch Station. The area is a vast stretch of land composed of blanket bog, lochans, rivers, and rocky outcrops which makes it a very challenging environment but which still supports varieties of flora and fauna. A wealth of plants, insect, bird and animal life can be seen here ranging from curlews and grouse to roe and red deer. One of the best ways to sample the stark beauty of this unique area is to take a train journey on the famous West Highland Railway, as the line crosses the moorland for 23 miles and in doing so rises to over 1,300 ft above sea level. *Gordon Edgar Collection/Rail Photoprints*

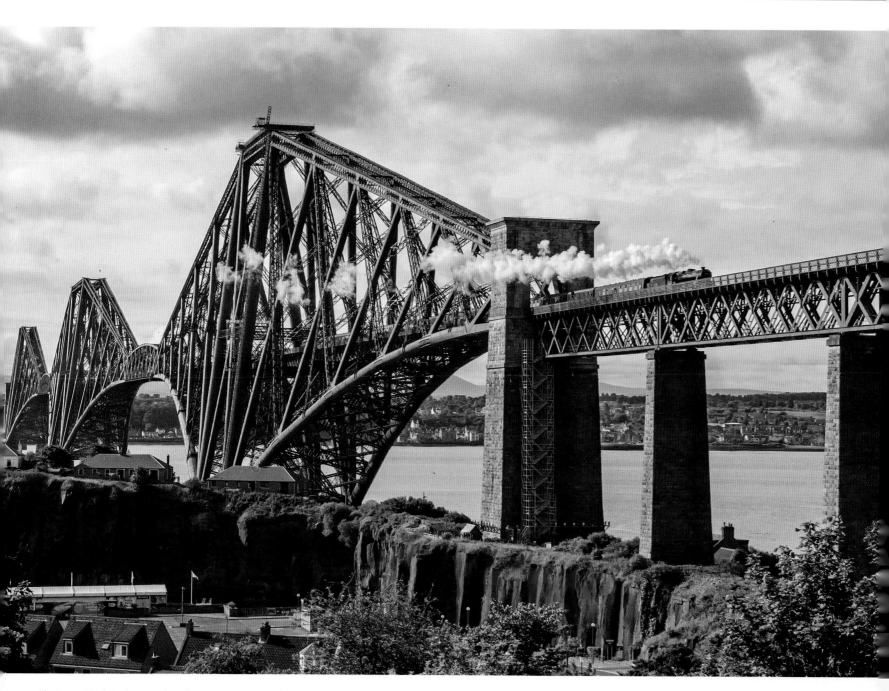

The iconic Forth Railway Bridge. This stunning image shows preserved Stanier 'Black Five' BR No 44871 working the Scottish Rail Preservation Society (SRPS) excursion from Linlithgow to Tweedbank via the Forth Bridge, Dunfermline, Kirkcaldy and Edinburgh. The locomotive is seen as it nears North Queensferry at 9:43am on 20 August 2017. In that year the SRPS excursion operated each Sunday for 4 weeks from 6 August, making this the third trip, the previous two having been headed by classmate BR No 45407 and the fourth also hauled by BR No 44871. *Greg Fitchett*

This image was first published in the online railway magazine *Railway Herald*, visit http://www.railwayherald.co.uk/

Stanier 'Black Five' BR No 44872 then allocated to Aston (3D) is seen double heading with Rebuilt 'Patriot' class BR No 45512 BUNSEN approaching Crewe with an up express, circa 1956. *Rail Photoprints Collection*

This Crewe Works built locomotive (Lot 174) entered traffic during March 1945 as LMS No 4872 and was withdrawn from Lostock Hall (10D) in September 1967. After a working life of 22 years, 6 months and 3 days it was cut up by J. McWilliams of Shettleston during March 1968.

GOODS TRAINS TO STOP
TO PIN DOWN BRAKES

Stanier 'Black Five' BR No 44873 then allocated to Saltley (21A) clambers over the, in this image, well-defined summit of the Lickey Incline at Blackwell with 1MO6 during May 1963, with the assistance of a banking engine. Note the painted-on shed identification marks. The Lickey Incline, south of Birmingham, is the steepest sustained main-line railway incline in Great Britain. The climb is a gradient of 1 in 37.7 for a continuous distance of two miles. It is located on the present day Cross Country Route between Barnt Green and Bromsgrove stations in Worcestershire. During the steam era some trains required the assistance of banking locomotives to ensure that the train reaches the top. *Rail Photoprints Collection*

This Crewe Works built locomotive (Lot 174) entered traffic during March 1945 as LMS No 4873 and was withdrawn from Springs Branch (8F) in November 1967. After a working life of 22 years, 8 months and 3 days it was cut up by Drapers of Hull during March 1968.

Stanier 'Black Five' BR No 44878 is seen at its home depot of Carlisle Kingmoor (68A), circa 1957. Note that the water tower can be seen to have coal braziers attached at the top to help prevent icing up of the horizontal section of the delivery pipe. Note also the blue Scottish smokebox number plate and the racing style bicycle 'holding up the water tower!'
*Rail Photoprints Collection*

This Crewe Works built locomotive (Lot 174) entered traffic during May 1945 as LMS No 4878 and was withdrawn from Lostock Hall (10D) in July 1968. After a working life of 23 years and 2 months it was cut up by Cohens of Kettering during February 1969.

Stanier 'Black Five' BR No 44879 then allocated to Carlisle Kingmoor (12A) is seen passing the locomotive depot at Perth (63A) with an unidentified southbound 4-coach passenger train on 9 May 1958. Note that the footplateman is doffing his cap to the crew of sister Carlisle Upperby allocated engine No 45451 (in the siding). *David Anderson*

This Crewe Works built locomotive (Lot 174) entered traffic during May 1945 as LMS No 4879 and was withdrawn from Perth in April 1967. After a working life of 21 years, 11 months and 1 day it was cut up by Motherwell Machinery & Scrap of Wishaw during September 1967.

Stanier 'Black Five' BR
No 44912 is seen at
Holbeck in the company
of 'A1' BR No 60117 BOIS
ROUSSEL and 'J50' Br
No 68892. *Len Mills*

This Crewe Works built locomotive (Lot 174) entered traffic during November 1945 as LMS No 4912 and was withdrawn from Holbeck (55A) in September 1967. After a working life of 21 years and 10 months it was cut up by Cashmores of Great Bridge during September 1968.

Stanier 'Black Five' BR
No 44915 then allocated
to Bletchley (1E) is seen
at Waterloo station on 24
May 1965. *Ian Turnbull/
Rail Photoprints*

This Crewe Works built locomotive (Lot 174) entered traffic during December 1945 as LMS No 4915 and was withdrawn from Lostock Hall (10D) in December 1967. After a working life of 21 years and 10 months it was cut up by T.W Ward of Sheffield during October 1968.

Stanier 'Black Five' BR No 44916 is seen on the WCML at Winwick during 1962. The then Longsight (9A) allocated locomotive has in tow two 'dead' unidentified members of the Gresley LNER 'V2' class and it can be assumed that those locomotives were making their final journey and a date with a cutting torch. *Colin Whitfield/Rail Photoprints*

This Crewe Works built locomotive (Lot 174) entered traffic during December 1945 as LMS No 4916 and was withdrawn from Stockport Edgeley (9B) in December 1967. After a working life of 21 years it was cut up by Drapers of Hull during February 1968.

Stanier 'Black Five' BR No 44918 then allocated to Nottingham (16D) is seen at Lincoln Central with the Railway Correspondence and Travel Society (RCTS) East Midlands Branch Nottingham and Lincolnshire area rail tour 1X28, on 12 September 1964. The tour started and finished at Nottingham Midland and included various visits to branch lines and sidings some of which were hauled by diesel locomotives D3619 and D3620 respectively. *Rail Photoprints Collection*

This Crewe Works built locomotive (Lot 174) entered traffic during December 1945 as LMS No 4918 and was withdrawn from Trafford Park (9E) in January 1967. After a working life of 21 years, 1 month and 1 day it was cut up by Cashmores of Great Bridge during July 1967.

Stanier 'Black Five' BR No 44920 then allocated to Saltley (21A) is seen with a Bristol-Birmingham train cresting the taxing climb from Bromsgrove at Blackwell whilst double heading with an unidentified BR 'Standard 5MT' on 4 October 1958. Note that the pair still required the assistance of a banking engine which would cease 'pushing' on reaching the summit and in all probability, use the points and signals seen to the left of the lead engine to return to Bromsgrove. *Mike Morant Collection*

This Crewe Works built locomotive (Lot 174) entered traffic during December 1945 as LMS No 4920 and was withdrawn from Springs Branch (8F) in November 1967. After a working life of 21 years, 11 months and 1 day it was cut up by Drapers of Hull during March 1968.

## 44932–44943 September–December, 12 locomotives built at Horwich Works
Introduced with Domed Boilers, Sloping Throatplates and 28 element Superheaters. Boilers built at Crewe, locomotive wheelbase 27ft 2in.

Preserved Stanier 'Black Five' BR No 44932 with a Carnforth (10A) shed code is seen at Skipton with a 'Waverley' headboard during August 2010. The charter train was a York-Carlisle via Settle Junction and the S&C route return service with 1Z80 outward and 1Z81 in bound, BR No 44932 used on both legs. *Fred Kerr*

This Horwich Works built locomotive (Lot 174) entered traffic during September 1945 as LMS No 4932 and was withdrawn from Rose Grove (10F) in August 1968. After a working life of 22 years and 11 months it was saved for preservation with a sloping throat plate domed boiler, 28 element superheater and top feed on second ring of boiler barrel.

After being bought direct from British Railways for preservation BR No 44932 became a popular locomotive appearing regularly on the national network mainlines, between overhauls. As can be seen in the image below, the engine actually became a 'Green Five' in the early days of preservation (lined Brunswick Green livery) which it never carried in BR service. No 44932 was withdrawn August 1968 coinciding with the end of steam on British Railway metals and moved to Carnforth following its purchase as part of the establishment of the then Steamtown Museum. Whilst Steamtown was open, and once the ban on operating steam trains on the main line was lifted in 1972, Carnforth was used as a base to operate trains to York and to Sellafield. There were however test runs, the first destination for those being Ulverston, alternately hauled by BR No 44871 and BR No 44932. Those trips preceded connecting special trains to Barrow in Furness. Steamtown was originally established by the well-known railway preservationist Dr. Peter Beet (1937–2005) with financial support from Sir Bill McAlpine. In 1974 McAlpine became a shareholder and subsequently acquired a controlling interest in the company, Steamtown closed in 1997. When Steamtown closed BR No 44932 moved to the Midland Steam Centre (MRC) at Butterley where it was completely overhauled. Later that year, the former Steamtown site was purchased by locomotive restorer David Smith, who owns the West Coast Railway Company (WCRC) which currently has its major locomotive storage and operating base there. By 2010, the 'Black Five' was owned by David Smith and happily back in operation on the main line. Since then it continued to operate charter trains, often from the West Coast Railway Company base at Southall and also North of the Border. The locomotive's main line certificate was valid until 2017, and the boiler certificate to 2020, notwithstanding that the locomotive in 2018 was reportedly undergoing an overhaul at Carnforth.

Preserved Stanier 'Black Five' BR No 44932 is seen in BR Express Brunswick Green livery with the 2nd train of the first steam special between Steamtown and Ulverston during September 1972. *Photographer unknown but appreciated*

Stanier 'Black Five' BR No 44933 then allocated to Newton Heath (26A) picks up water from Moore troughs as it heads south with an up local, circa 1949. Note the water supply for the troughs visible behind the train. *R.A. Whitfield/Rail Photoprints*

This Horwich Works built locomotive (Lot 174) entered traffic during October 1945 as LMS No 4933 and was withdrawn from Edge Hill (8A) in October 1967. After a working life of 21 years it was cut up by Cashmores of Great Bridge during May 1968.

Stanier 'Black Five' BR No 44935 then allocated to Llandudno Junction (6G) is seen at Chester 1959 with smartly lined out livery whilst waiting to depart with a train for Crewe.
*R.A. Whitfield/Rail Photoprints*

This Horwich Works built locomotive (Lot 174) entered traffic during October 1945 as LMS No 4935 and was withdrawn from Warrington Dallam (8B) in October 1966. After a working life of 20 years it was cut up by Cashmores of Great Bridge during April 1967.

Stanier 'Black Five' BR No 44937 then allocated to Carlisle Upperby (12B) is seen climbing towards Shap with a northbound fitted freight, circa 1963. Shap Summit is a well-known section of the West Coast Main Line. It has a 1:75 gradient for trains heading north, and in the steam era banking engines from Tebay were often used to assist trains. *Jim Carter/Rail Photoprints*

This Horwich Works built locomotive (Lot 174) entered traffic during November 1945 as LMS No 4937 and was withdrawn from Carlisle Kingmoor (12A) in May 1967. After a working life of 20 years, 5 months and 30 days it was cut up by J. McWilliams of Shettleston during November 1967.

Stanier 'Black Five' BR No 44938 then allocated to Newton Heath is seen approaching Macclesfield with a London via Stoke on Trent express. Note the period advertising hoardings. *Jim Carter/Rail Photoprints*

This Horwich Works built locomotive (Lot 174) entered traffic during November 1945 as LMS No 4938 and was withdrawn from Newton Heath (9D) in October 1967. After a working life of 20 years, 10 months and 30 days it was cut up by Cashmores of Great Bridge during March 1968.

Stanier 'Black Five' LMS No 4940 then allocated to Newton Heath (26A), BR No 44940 is seen arriving at Preston from the Fylde Coast in early BR days. However, the locomotive in this May 1949 image is still sporting LMS (LMSR) livery. The train has just passed under Ashton Street bridge and is about to pass St. Walburge's Church on the approach to Fylde Junction, just to the north of the station. Note the vintage carriage behind the tender (possibly ex Lancashire & Yorkshire Railway). On the embankment two gentlemen are seen visiting the roughly built pigeon loft, but it seems only one of them is interested in the passing train. *Mike Morant Collection*

This Horwich Works built locomotive (Lot 174) entered traffic during November 1945 as LMS No 4940 and was withdrawn from Stockport Edgeley (9B) in March 1968. After a working life of 21 years, 3 months and 29 days it was cut up by Drapers of Hull during August 1968.

# 1946

## 44921–44931 January–April, 11 locomotives built at Crewe Works
Introduced with Domed Boilers, Sloping Throatplates and 28 element Superheaters, locomotive wheelbase 27ft 2in.

Stanier 'Black Five' BR No 44921 then allocated to Perth (63A) waits to leave Glasgow Buchanan Street with the down 'Saint Mungo' for Aberdeen, on 3 April 1961. The 'Saint Mungo' Glasgow Buchanan Street –Aberdeen first ran on 5 July 1937, on the closure of Buchanan Street station the train ran from Glasgow Queen Street (November 1966). The title was suspended on 8 September 1939 and reinstated 23 May 1949 with the last titles run taking place on 4 May 1968. St. Mungo is the patron saint of Glasgow. *Sid Rickard J & J Collection/Rail Photoprints*

This Crewe Works built locomotive (Lot 174) entered traffic during January 1946 as LMS No 4921 and was withdrawn from Perth in February 1965. After a working life of 19 years and 1 month it was cut up by P&W McLellan of Bo'ness during June 1965.

Stanier 'Black Five' BR No 44922 then allocated to St. Rollox (BR 65B-LMSR 31A) also referred to as Balornock, is seen double heading with sister locomotive BR No 45389 (Armstrong Whitworth 1937). The pair are raising the echoes on the steep climb out of Oban terminus station towards Glencruitten summit with the 12:09pm Oban–Glasgow and Edinburgh Princes Street passenger service on 20 September 1957. The driver seems to be enjoying the occasion as he looks towards the camera. *David Anderson*

This Crewe Works built locomotive (Lot 174) entered traffic during January 1946 as LMS No 4922 and was withdrawn from St. Rollox where it was allocated for the whole of its BR working life in May 1964. After a working life of 18 years, 3 months and 30 days it was cut up by Connels of Coatbridge during November 1964.

Stanier 'Black Five' BR No 44923 then allocated to St. Rollox (65B) is seen with an up freight working on a single line section north of Callander on 3 July 1957 whilst coupled with a self-weighing tender. The tender was one of four coal weighing vehicles which ran attached to various 'Black Five' locomotives for test purposes. *David Anderson*

This Crewe Works built locomotive (Lot 174) entered traffic during January 1946 as LMS No 4923 and was withdrawn from St. Rollox in June 1964. After a working life of 18 years and 5 months it was cut up by Motherwell Machinery & Scrap of Wishaw during October 1964.

The purpose of self-weighing tenders was to measure coal consumption. The coal bunker was a separate unit suspended on pivots which were connected to a steelyard at the rear of the unit. The whole assembly could be 'fixed' when the loco was working and released when it was necessary to weigh the contents. *Keith Langston Collection*

Stanier 'Black Five' BR No 44927 then allocated Blackpool (24E) simmers alongside the shed of its home depot, circa 1957. The boiler details and motion are seen to good effect in this image. *Rail Photoprints Collection*

This Crewe Works built locomotive (Lot 174) entered traffic during February 1946 as LMS No 4927 and was withdrawn from Bolton (9K) in September 1967. After a working life of 21 years and 7 months it was cut up by Cashmores of Newport during February 1968.

## 44944–44966 January–August, 23 locomotives built at Horwich Works
Introduced with Domed Boilers, Sloping Throatplates and 28 element Superheaters, locomotive wheelbase 27ft 2in. Boilers built at Crewe.

Stanier 'Black Five' BR No 44947 then allocated to Bolton (9K) is seen at its home depot in the company of BR No 45104 (Vulcan Foundry 1935), both were in light steam on 29 March 1968. Note that the smoke box numberplates and shed plates have been removed and replaced with hand painted replicas, and that both locomotives have the depot name stencilled on their front buffer beams. *Rail Photoprints Collection*

This Horwich Works built locomotive (Lot 174) entered traffic during February 1946 as LMS No 4947 and was withdrawn from Bolton in June 1968. After a working life of 22 years and 4 months it was cut up by Cohens of Kettering during October 1968.

Stanier 'Black Five' BR No 44956 then allocated to Carstairs (64D) is seen piloting 'B1' class BR No 61404 with a Glasgow to Edinburgh Waverley service whilst passing Haymarket Central Junction on 12 October 1958. Note the top feed of a replacement boiler is located on the forward ring of the barrel. *David Anderson*

This Horwich Works built locomotive (Lot 174) entered traffic during April 1946 as LMS No 4956 and was withdrawn from Carstairs in June 1966. After a working life of 20 years and 2 months it was cut up by J. McWilliams of Shettleston during October 1966.

Stanier 'Black Five' as LMS No 4956 then allocated to St. Rollox (BR 65B-LMSR 31A) also referred to as Balornock depot. The image was taken circa 1947 and is just outside the aforementioned depot with the locomotive waiting to reverse under the bridge and onto the ash-pits and coaling stage. As BR No 44956 this 'Black Five' spent all of its BR working life allocated to Scottish sheds. There was much swopping of boilers during the working lives of the class however, this locomotive is seen configured in the manner it first entered traffic. In this image Stanier's Belpaire firebox and tapered boiler design combination can be seen to good effect. Note also the filler pipes for the sand boxes and the fact that in this instance the water pipe to the top feed is on the outside of the boiler cladding. *Mike Morant Collection*

Stanier 'Black Five' BR No 44960 then allocated to Perth (63A) is seen shunting an additional coach onto its train at Ballinluig Junction in July 1957. The single-line tablet catcher can be seen attached to the cab side. *David Anderson*

This Horwich Works built locomotive (Lot 174) entered traffic during May 1946 as LMS No 4960 and was withdrawn from Perth in January 1966. After a working life of 19 years, 8 months and 1 day it was cut up by J. McWilliams of Shettleston during June 1966.

Deputising for a failed diesel unit Stanier 'Black Five' BR No 44961 the allocated Perth (63A) stands at Crieff station having worked in with the 11.01 service from Gleneagles on 28 March 1964. *Ian Turnbull/Rail Photoprints*

This Horwich Works built locomotive (Lot 174) entered traffic during June 1946 as LMS No 4961 and was withdrawn from Perth in June 1964, having been allocated there for the whole of the BR period. After a working life of 17 years, 11 months and 16 days it was cut up by Motherwell Machinery & Scrap of Wishaw during September 1964.

Stanier 'Black Five' LMS No 4966 then allocated to Saltley (21A) is seen at Horwich Works circa 1947, coupled to a self-weighing tender. The Peel Monument, also known as Holcombe Tower (a memorial to Sir Robert Peel) overlooks Rivington and Horwich and is faintly visible on the top of Holcombe Hill above the locomotive cab. *Mike Morant Collection*

This Horwich Works built locomotive (Lot 174) entered traffic during August 1946 as LMS No 4966 and was withdrawn from Shrewsbury (6D) in September 1966. After a working life of 20 years and 1 month it was cut up by Cashmores of Great Bridge during January 1967.

Stanier 'Black Five' BR No 44966 then allocated to Saltley passes through Kemble station with an up train of vans on 7 February 1964. Note the change here sign for Cirencester and Tetbury. *Hugh Ballantyne/ Rail Photoprints*

## 44967-44981 April-July, 15 locomotives built at Crewe Works
Introduced with Domed Boilers, Sloping Throatplates and 28 element Superheaters, locomotive wheelbase 27ft 2in.

Stanier 'Black Five' BR No 44967 then allocated to Eastfield (65A) climbs through Glen Falloch with a West Highland Line freight, circa 1957. Note the different capacity and style ESSO tank vehicles. *John Day Collection/Rail Photoprints*

This Crewe Works built locomotive (Lot 183) entered traffic during April 1946 as LMS No 4967 and was withdrawn from Dumfries (67E) in May 1964. After a working life of 18 years and 30 days it was cut up by Connels of Coatbridge during September 1964.

Stanier 'Black Five' BR No 44968 then allocated to Eastfield (65A) is seen at Crianlarich (Upper) station with the 1.20pm passenger working from Mallaig and Fort William. The locomotive is taking water prior to heading the 5.23pm departure for Glasgow Queen Street, during the summer of 1960. *David Anderson*

This Crewe Works built locomotive (Lot 183) entered traffic during April 1946 as LMS No 4968 and was withdrawn from Motherwell (66B) in May 1964. After a working life of 18 years and 30 days it was cut up by Connels of Coatbridge during November 1964.

Stanier 'Black Five' BR No 44973 then allocated to Carstairs (66E) is seen on the WCML at Carluke with a local passenger service during June 1965. *Rail Photoprints Collection*

This Crewe Works built locomotive (Lot 183) entered traffic during May 1946 as LMS No 4973 and was withdrawn from Carstairs in September 1965 having been allocated to Scottish depots for the whole of the BR period. After a working life of 19 years, 4 months and 1 day it was cut up by Motherwell Machinery & Scrap of Wishaw during December 1965.

Stanier 'Black Five' BR No 44975 then allocated to Dalry Road (64C) passes Bishopbriggs with an eastbound rake of three ESSO oil tanks, note the mineral wagons acting as barrier vehicles behind the tender and in front of the guard's van, circa 1963. Note the Wimpey Homes sign and new building site above and to the left of the locomotive. *J & J Collection – Sid Rickard/Rail Photoprints*

This Crewe Works built locomotive (Lot 183) entered traffic during May 1946 as LMS No 4975 and was withdrawn from Dalry Road in September 1965 having been allocated to Scottish depots for the whole of the BR period. After a working life of 19 years, 4 months and 1 day it was cut up by Motherwell Machinery & Scrap of Wishaw during January 1966.

Stanier 'Black Five' BR No 44978 then allocated to Perth (63A) is seen standing in the yard at Aberfeldy the terminus of the branch line from Ballinluig, with a weedkilling train on 5 July 1957. Note the tablet catcher equipment located on the cab side. The station was opened in 1865 by the Inverness & Perth Junction Railway and closed to freight in March 1965, and passenger traffic in May 1965. *David Anderson*

This Crewe Works built locomotive (Lot 183) entered traffic during June 1946 as LMS No 4978 and was withdrawn from Perth in July 1965 having been allocated to Scottish depots for the whole of the BR period. After a working life of 19 years and 15 days it was cut up by Arnott Young of Old Kilpatrick during November 1965.

Stanier 'Black Five' BR No 44981 then allocated to Kentish Town (14B) is seen leaving Barrow on Soar with a down semi-fast passenger service, on 1 June 1953. Note the loading gauge maximum height indicator bar suspended above the line to the siding (loading area). Basically, if the loaded railway vehicle passed clear of the indicator bar then it would be sure to pass below all the other structures on the line. A tall signal box with steep steps can be seen beyond the footbridge. *Dave Cobbe Collection/Rail Photoprints*

This Crewe Works built locomotive (Lot 183) entered traffic during July 1946 as LMS No 4981 and was withdrawn from Shrewsbury (6D) in January 1967. After a working life of 20 years, 6 months and 1 day it was cut up by Cashmores of Newport during October 1967.

## 44982-44991 September–December, 10 locomotives built at Horwich Works
Introduced with Domed Boilers, Sloping Throatplates and 28 element Superheaters, locomotive wheelbase 27ft 2in. Boilers built at Crewe.

Stanier 'Black Five BR No 44984 then allocated to Colwick (16B) takes water at Rugby Central with the 17.15 Nottingham Victoria-Marylebone passenger train on the last day of through services, 3 September 1966. Note the wreath on the smoke-box and members of the local community who had assembled to mark the passing! *Rail Photoprints Collection*

This Horwich Works built locomotive (Lot 183) entered traffic during September 1946 as LMS No 4984 and was withdrawn from Colwick (16B) in November 1966. After a working life of 20 years and 2 months it was cut up by Cashmores of Great Bridge during March 1967.

Stanier 'Black Five' BR No 44987 then allocated to Carnforth (10A) is seen after arriving at Bridlington with the 08.20 from Bradford Exchange, on 14 August 1965. Note the presumably holidaying family complete with pet dog. The footplateman and his train have elicited a 'double teapot' stance from the on-duty station master. *Ian Turnbull/Rail Photoprints*

This Horwich Works built locomotive (Lot 183) entered traffic during November 1946 as LMS No 4987 and was withdrawn from Carnforth in October 1966. After a working life of 19 years, 10 months and 30 days it was cut up by Cashmores of Great Bridge during February 1967.

# 1947

## 44992-44999 January-March, 8 locomotives built at Horwich Works

Introduced with Domed Boilers, Sloping Throatplates and 28 element Superheaters, locomotive wheelbase 27ft 2in. Boilers built at Crewe.

Stanier 'Black Five' BR No 44994 then allocated to Dalry Road (64C) is seen when about to leave Stirling station with a stopping passenger working to Edinburgh Princes Street station in June 1961. Note that at this time the locomotive carried a domed boiler with the top feed on the front ring of the boiler barrel, and note also the Diesel shunter in an adjacent platform to the right. *David Anderson*

This Horwich Works built locomotive (Lot 183) entered traffic during January 1947 as LMS No 4994 and was withdrawn from Dalry Road in July 1964. After a working life of 17 years, 5 months and 30 days it was cut up by Arnott Young of Old Kilpatrick during November 1964.

Stanier 'Black Five' BR No 44997 is seen at Perth (63A) the locomotives then home depot (10/01/48 – 01/05/67) prior to working a leg of the 'Granite City' special working Edinburgh Waverley – Aberdeen, on Easter Saturday 25 March 1967. The also named 'British Rail (Scottish Region) Grand Scottish Tour No.1' was a combined steam and diesel hauled 18 coach train, with steam in the form of this 'Black Five' and 'A4' Pacific BR No 60009 UNION OF SOUTH AFRICA taking over from diesel power at Perth. After a further diesel hauled section the two steam locomotives took charge of the final leg from Perth to Edinburgh Waverley. And all for the princely sum of 50 shillings, £2.50 in modern money! BR No 44997 was built with a domed boiler with a top feed on the second ring of the boiler barrel. *Rail Photoprints*

For additional information on rail tours see www.sixbellsjunction.co.uk/

This Horwich Works built locomotive (Lot 187) entered traffic during March 1947 as LMS No 4997 and was withdrawn from Perth in May 1967. After a working life of 20 years, 2 months and 2 days it was cut up by J. McWilliams of Shettleston during September 1967.

## 44783-44799 March-October, 17 locomotives built at Horwich Works

Introduced with Domed Boilers, Sloping Throatplates and 28 element Superheaters, locomotive wheelbase 27ft 2in. Boilers built at Crewe.

'Black Fives' were the most common type of locomotives to work on main line Highlands trains during the last twenty-five years of the steam era. They regularly hauled trains between Perth and Inverness and Inverness and Wick, with no less than 35 of the 'Class 5' 4-6-0s being allocated to Inverness in 1942. In 1946 a new 54ft turntable was installed at Kyle of Lochalsh, which allowed 'Black Fives' to work the Kyle line for the first time (locomotive and tender wheelbase length 53ft 2¾in). That turntable is now installed and operational at Aviemore on the Strathspey Railway.

In Britain, where steam hauled trains generally had vacuum operated brakes, it was quite common for turntables to be operated by vacuum motors worked from the locomotive's vacuum ejector or pump via a flexible hose or pipe, although a few manually and electrically operated examples existed. The major turntable manufacturers were Ransomes and Rapier, Ipswich and Cowans Sheldon, Carlisle. For more information visit www.strathspeyrailway.co.uk/

This Horwich Works built locomotive (Lot 187) entered traffic during April 1947 as LMS No 4785 and was withdrawn from Corkerhill (67A) in June 1964. After a working life of 17 years and 2 months it was cut up by Motherwell Machinery & Scrap of Wishaw during September 1964.

Stanier 'Black Five' BR No 44785 with an Inverness shed code (60A) is seen on the turntable adjacent to Kyle of Lochalsh station in this 1960s image. Note the snow plough. This locomotive would reverse off the turntable.
*David Anderson*

Stanier 'Black Five' BR No 44794 then allocated to Perth (63A) and with a tender full of steam coal leaves Bridge of Dun with the 12.25 Perth – Aberdeen parcels service, on 29 June 1966. *Brian Robbins/Rail Photoprints*

This Horwich Works built locomotive (Lot 187) entered traffic during August 1947 as LMS No 4794 and was withdrawn from Perth in April 1967 having been allocated to Scottish depots for the whole of the BR period. After a working life of 19 years and 8 months it was cut up by Motherwell Machinery & Scrap of Wishaw during September 1967.

Stanier 'Black Five' BR No 44794 is seen at Aberdeen station with the 12.00 service to Glasgow Buchanan Street, during May 1966. The self-cleaning smokebox (SC) plate is clearly visible below the shedplate which appears to be blank, although at the time the locomotive was allocated to Perth. *Ian Turnbull/Rail Photoprints*

A 'Self Cleaning' smokebox was basically comprised of a robust mesh grille, which formed a filter between the front tubeplate and the exhaust. Any large pieces of char/ash passing through the boiler tubes therefore tended to be broken up on impact with the mesh, thus creating finer particles which were swept up the chimney instead of accumulating in the bottom of the smokebox. This device did not negate the need to clean out the smokebox but reduced the amount of work that had to be done.

Stanier 'Black Five' BR No 44798 then allocated to Inverness (60A) is seen between duties at Perth during June 1956. Note that in this instance the cab-side number is in the higher position often preferred by Scottish depots (and St Rollox Works) accordingly the figure 5 power classification symbol is shown below the number and also the early British Railways tender markings. *David Anderson*

This Horwich Works built locomotive (Lot 187) entered traffic during October 1947 as LMS No 4798 and was withdrawn from Corkerhill (67A) in September 1966 having been allocated to Scottish depots for the whole of the BR period. After a working life of 18 years, 11 months and 1 day it was cut up by J. McWilliams of Shettleston during January 1967.

British Railways shed codes were used to identify the engine sheds that its locomotives were allocated to for maintenance purposes. The former London, Midland and Scottish Railway (LMS) alpha-numeric system was extended to cover all regions and used until replaced by alphabetic codes in 1973. Each steam locomotive was allocated to a particular shed and an oval, cast metal plate (usually 4⅝ in x 7½ in) with the depot code bolted to the smokebox door.

From 1950 onwards, the numbers to regional allocations were as follows:

*1–28 London Midland Region. 30–41 Eastern Region. 50–56 North Eastern Region. 60–68 Scottish Region. 70–75 Southern Region. 81–89 Western Region.*

A line up of Stanier 4-6-0 locomotives seen at Perth (63A) on 5 July 1957, their home depot. From left to right Derby 1943 built 'Black Five' BR No 45472, 'Jubilee' class 6P5F BR No 45673 KEPPEL (1935 Crewe) and 'Black Five' BR No 44798. Note the differing boiler top feed positions on the 'Black Five' engines. *David Anderson*

## 44758-44764 September–November, 7 locomotives built at Crewe Works

Introduced with Domed Boilers, Sloping Throatplates and 28 element Superheaters. Fitted with Timken Roller Bearings throughout (Ivatt modifications).

In order to accommodate the housings of the Timken roller-bearings, these locomotives were constructed with a longer wheelbase, 27ft 6in instead of 27ft 2in and also a change in the coupled wheelbase, 7ft + 8ft to 7ft+ 8ft 4in. These increases ensured that the bearing housings did not foul the locomotives ashpan.

Stanier 'Black Five' BR No 44759 then allocated to Crewe South (5B) stands at Crewe Works after overhaul, during February 1965. Note the overhead electric cables warning stickers and the top feed located on the front ring of the boiler barrel and that the associated feed pipe is within the cladding and covered by a metal strip. *Rail Photoprints Collection*

This Crewe Works built locomotive (Lot 187) entered traffic during September 1947 as LMS No 4759 and was withdrawn from Carlisle Kingmoor (12A) in November 1967. After a working life of 20 years and 2 months, it was cut up by Motherwell Machinery & Scrap of Wishaw during March 1968.

Stanier 'Black Five' BR No 44762 then allocated to Crewe North (5A) approaches Wigan with a rake of vans, during April 1962. *J. R. Carter/Rail Photoprints*

This Crewe Works built locomotive (Lot 187) entered traffic during October 1947 as LMS No 4762 and was withdrawn from Croes Newydd (6C) in November 1966. After a working life of 19 years, 1 month and 1 day, it was cut up by Drapers of Hull during April 1967.

## 44765-44766 December, 2 locomotives built Crewe Works

Introduced with Domed Boilers, Sloping Throatplates and 28 element Superheaters. Fitted with Timken Roller Bearings throughout. Additionally, locomotives 44765, and 44766 were fitted with double blastpipes and chimneys (Ivatt modifications). In order to accommodate the housings of the Timken roller-bearings, these locomotives were constructed with a longer wheelbase, 27ft 6in instead of 27ft 2in and also a change in the coupled wheelbase, 7ft + 8ft to 7ft+ 8ft 4in. These increases ensured that the bearing housings did not foul the locomotives ashpan.

Stanier 'Black Five' BR No 44766 with double chimney and at that time allocated to Bescot (21B) is seen at its home depot on 6 May 1962. *Ian Turnbull/Rail Photoprints*

This Crewe Works built locomotive (Lot 187) entered traffic during December 1947 as LMS No 4766 and was withdrawn from Crewe South in August 1967. After a working life of 19 years, 8 months and 1 day, it was cut up by Cashmores of Newport during December 1967.

Stanier 'Black Five' BR No 44766 is seen at Crewe South (5B) its then home depot in May 1967. *John Chalcraft Rail/Photoprints*

## 44767 December, 1 locomotive built Crewe Works

Introduced with Domed Boiler, Sloping Throatplate and 28 element Superheater. This George Ivatt modified locomotive was fitted with Timken Roller Bearings throughout. Originally fitted with double blastpipe and chimney which was removed in 1953. BR No 44767 (LMS 4767) was the only member of the class built with 'Outside' Stephenson valve gear, it is unique in that this type of valve gear was normally fitted between the frames of an engine. Prior to this the last British locomotive fitted with outside Stephenson valve gear was a GWR single wheeler, back in 1884. In order to accommodate the housings of the Timken roller-bearings, the locomotive was constructed with a longer wheelbase, 27ft 6in instead of 27ft 2in and also a change in the coupled wheelbase, 7ft + 8ft to 7ft+ 8ft 4in. These increases ensured that the bearing housings did not foul the locomotives ashpan. The modifications included electric lighting.

Unique Stanier 'Black Five' BR No 44767 then allocated to Carlisle Kingmoor (12A) with outside Stephenson valve gear is seen at Glasgow Polmadie depot in June 1954. The Stephenson valve gear can be clearly identified in this image. *Rail Photoprints Collection*

This Crewe Works built locomotive (Lot 187) entered traffic during December 1947 as LMS No 4767 and was withdrawn from Carlisle Kingmoor in December 1967. After a working life of 20 years it was saved for preservation with a top feed on forward barrel of the boiler.

Stanier 'Black Five' BR No 44767 then allocated to Carlisle Kingmoor (12A) is seen shunting a BR Standard 'Mogul' locomotive at Patricroft depot, during April 1965. *Jim Carter-Steve Armitage Archive/Rail Photoprints*

In the United Kingdom, locomotives having Stephenson valve gear normally had it mounted in between the locomotive's frames. The LMS built 'Black Five' locomotives were fitted with Walschaerts' valve gear as standard. However, BR No 44767 (LMS 4767) was experimentally fitted with Stephenson valve gear mounted outside the wheels and frames. Instead of eccentrics, double return cranks were used to drive the eccentric rods, and a launch-type expansion link was used. The aim of the experiment was to find out if a valve gear having variable lead (as opposed to the constant lead of the Walschaerts' motion) would improve performance. On trial, it proved to have no big advantage, although in normal service it did gain a reputation with engine crews for being a good performer on banks (gradients). The Stephenson gear reportedly added £600 more to the cost of the build.

BR No 44767 was privately bought by Ian Storey and was stored at Carnforth until 1974, when it was taken to Thornaby for restoration by North Eastern Locomotive Preservation Group (NELPG). Restoration work was completed in time for the 150th anniversary of the Stockton and Darlington Railway in 1975. The former Secretary of State for Northern Ireland, William Whitelaw named BR No 44767 after famous railway engineer George Stephenson at Shildon. A plaque below its nameplates reads:

*This locomotive was named by the Right Hon. William Whitelaw CH MC MP at Shildon*
*on August 25th 1975 to commemorate the 150th anniversary of the Stockton and Darlington Railway.*

The locomotive saw regular use on mainline charters throughout the UK. The locomotive was based on the North Yorkshire Moors Railway (NYMR) before being taken out of service at the end of 2002 for a full overhaul. In December 2009 the locomotive returned to steam and moved to the Great Central Railway (GCR) for running in and painting. In the years up to and including 2014 the locomotive visited various steam railway locations before being withdrawn in early 2015 and moved to the Midland Railway Centre at Butterley in order to be restored to mainline operating standard. That work was reportedly ongoing in 2017.

Preserved Stanier 'Black Five' LMS No 4767 is seen at Grosmont NYMR during May 1981. In preservation the outside Stephenson valve gear fitted unique 'Black Five' carries the name GEORGE STEPHENSON. In LMS/BR service the engine was un-named. Note the Bank Hall (27A) shedplate from the period 30/11/50 – 30/03/62. *Keith Langston Collection*

The unique preserved Stanier 'Black Five' BR No 44767 passes Mallaig Junction Yard as it leaves Fort William with the 11.05 Fort William–Mallaig service, on 25 June 1986. In addition to the Stephenson valve gear the locomotive was originally fitted with experimental electric lighting. In this restoration era image, a lighting generator can be seen on the running plate alongside the smoke box. Note the spurious Fort William (65J) shedplate carried on this occasion, although Carlisle Kingmoor is stencilled on the buffer beam. *John Chalcraft/ Rail Photoprints*

## 44768-44782 April-August, 15 locomotives built at Crewe Works
Introduced with Domed Boilers, Sloping Throatplates and 28 element Superheaters, locomotive wheelbase 27ft 2in.

Stanier 'Black Five' BR No 44770 then allocated to Crewe North (5A) is seen at Cricklewood between duties, during September 1957. Note the domed boiler with top feed located on the forward ring of the barrel. *Rail Photoprints Collection*

This Crewe Works built locomotive (Lot 187) entered traffic during April 1947 as LMS No 4770 and was withdrawn from Carlisle Kingmoor (12A) in October 1967. After a working life of 20 years, 5 months and 30 days it was cut up by J. McWilliams of Shettleston during February 1968.

Stanier 'Black Five' BR No 44772 with a slightly out of focus Edge Hill (8A) shedplate, is seen arriving at Crewe with a down passenger service, 1962. Note the overhead electric equipment. *Alan H. Bryant ARPS/ Rail Photoprints*

This Crewe Works built locomotive (Lot 187) entered traffic during May 1947 as LMS No 4772 and was withdrawn from Edge Hill in October 1967. After a working life of 20 years and 5 months it was cut up by Cashmores of Newport during May 1968.

As part of the 1955 modernisation plan, the West Coast Mainline (WCML) was electrified in stages between 1959 and 1974. The first stretch to be electrified was Crewe to Manchester Piccadilly, completed on 12 September 1960. This was followed by Crewe to Liverpool Lime Street, completed on 1 January 1962. Electrification was then extended south to London Euston. The first electric trains from London ran on 12 November 1965, with full public service from 18 April 1966. Electrification of the Birmingham line was completed on 6 March 1967. In March 1970 the government approved electrification between Weaver Junction (where the route to Liverpool diverges) and Glasgow Central, and that work was completed on 6 May 1974.

Stanier 'Black Five' BR No 44773 then allocated to Chester (6A) is seen at Crewe station, whilst backing down to the North shed in August 1957, and in doing so passing under the North Bridge a location popular with railway enthusiasts. In fact, this author spent the majority of that month on 'the bridge', having travelled there from Mid-Cheshire on the push-pull service then known by most local schoolboys as the 'Dodger'. Happy days! *Rail Photoprints Collection*

This Crewe Works built locomotive (Lot 187) entered traffic during May 1947 as LMS No 4773 and was withdrawn from Edge Hill in December 1967. After a working life of 20 years and 7 months it was cut up by Cohens of Kettering during May 1968.

Stanier 'Black Five' BR No 44775 is seen at its then home depot Saltley (21A) December 1962. Note that at this time the locomotive had a top feed located on the centre ring of the boiler barrel. *Rail Photoprints Collection*

This Crewe Works built locomotive (Lot 187) entered traffic during June 1947 as LMS No 4775 and was withdrawn from Carlisle Kingmoor (12A) in October 1967. After a working life of 20 years, 3 months and 30 days it was cut up by J. McWilliams of Shettleston during March 1968.

Stanier 'Black Five' BR No 44777 then allocated to Tyseley (2A) is partially seen inside the shed at Saltley in 1966. Note the two Stanier '8F's' and the Ransomes & Rapier turntable. *Brian Robbins/Rail Photoprints*

Stanier 'Black Five' BR No 44781 then allocated to Carnforth (10A) with sister engine BR No 45046 is seen approaching Dove Holes on 27 April 1968 with 1Z77 'North West Rail Tour charter train'. *Rail Photoprints Collection*

This Crewe Works built locomotive (Lot 187) entered traffic during June 1947 as LMS No 4777 and was withdrawn from Patricroft (9H) in June 1968. After a working life of 21 years it was cut up by Cohens of Kettering during January 1969.

This Crewe Works built locomotive (Lot 187) entered traffic during August 1947 as LMS 4781. It was withdrawn from Carnforth in August 1968, after a working life of 21 years. The disposal information is inconclusive.

Stanier 'Black Five' BR No 44781 is seen heading train engine BR No 44871 (1945 Crewe built) whilst exiting Helm Tunnel on Sunday 11 August 1968. This British Rail Fifteen Guinea Special working was announced on the timing sheet as being the 'Last steam hauled train on British Railways standard gauge track' (1T57 throughout). Other locomotives used were the now preserved pair of 'Black Five' BR No 45110 and BR Standard 'Britannia' Pacific No 70013 OLIVER CROMWELL. *Chris Davies/ Rail Photoprints*

'Fifteen Guinea Special' itinerary shown below, courtesy of www.sixbellsjunction.co.uk

| Loco(s) | Route |
|---|---|
| 45110 | Liverpool Lime Street – Rainhill – Earlestown – Eccles – Deal Street – Manchester Victoria |
| 70013 | Manchester Victoria – Windsor Bridge No.1 – Windsor Bridge No.3 – Bolton – Darwen – Blackburn – Clitheroe – Hellifield – Settle Jn – (via S&C) – Petteril Bridge Jn – Carlisle |
| 44781 & 44871 | Carlisle – (reverse of outward route) – Manchester Victoria |
| 45110 | Manchester Victoria – (reverse of outward route) – Liverpool Lime Street |

# 1948

## 44698-44717 July-December, 20 locomotives built at Horwich Works

Introduced with Domed Boilers, Sloping Throatplates and 28 element Superheaters. Boilers built at Crewe. British Railways (BR) built locomotives. To simplify frame marking-off and machining the longer 27ft 6in wheelbase also, a change in the coupled wheelbase, 7ft + 8ft to 7ft+ 8ft 4in was adopted as standard for all locomotives in Lot Nos 192 and 199 irrespective of Valve motion and Axlebox bearing types (in this instance plain bearings). The smokeboxes were constructed to be 4in longer (all Ivatt modifications).

Stanier 'Black Five' BR No 44700 then allocated to Carstairs (64D) is seen having just passed the signal box at Beattock with a mixed freight train during April 1955. *David Anderson*

This Horwich Works BR built locomotive (Lot 192) entered traffic during July 1948 and was withdrawn from Carstairs in July 1966 having spent all of the BR era allocated to Scottish depots. After a working life of 17 years, 10 months and 30 days it was cut up by Motherwell Machinery & Scrap of Wishaw during October 1966.

Stanier 'Black Five' BR No 44700 is seen at Carstairs Junction with a local stopping train for Lanark on 3 May 1958. *David Anderson*

Stanier 'Black Five' BR No 44703 is seen on shed at its then home depot Aberdeen Ferryhill (61B) during October 1966 and in the company of the now preserved 'A2' class BR No 60532 BLUE PETER then a Dundee Tay Bridge allocated locomotive. *Brian Robbins/Rail Photoprints*

This Horwich Works BR built locomotive (Lot 192) entered traffic during August 1948 and was withdrawn from Eastfield (65A) in December 1966 having spent all of the BR era allocated to Scottish depots. After a working life of 18 years, 3 months and 2 days it was cut up by J. McWilliams of Shettleston during April 1967.

Stanier 'Black Five' BR No 44705 then allocated to Perth (63A) is seen at Forres shed on 2 September 1958. Note the tablet catcher fitted to cabside. *David Anderson*

This Horwich Works BR built locomotive (Lot 192) entered traffic during September 1948 and was withdrawn from Perth in September 1966 having spent all of the BR era allocated to Scottish depots. After a working life of 17 years, 11 months and 20 days it was cut up by J. McWilliams of Shettleston during December 1966.

Stanier 'Black Five' BR No 44708 then allocated to Chester (6A) with a train for Manchester is seen near Mickle Trafford, in this early BR era image dating from June 1949. *R. A. Whitfield/ Rail Photoprints*

This Horwich Works BR built locomotive (Lot 192) entered traffic during October 1948 and was withdrawn from Trafford Park in January 1968. After a working life of 19 years, 2 months and 29 days it was cut up by Cohens of Kettering during August 1968.

Stanier 'Black Five' BR No 44708 then allocated to Trafford Park (9E) arrives at Deganwy with the 14.00 Llandudno – Manchester Exchange service, on Saturday 22 August 1964. Note the holiday makers, and the obliging porter with a truck load of luggage. The station buildings are long gone but the signal box visible in this image was still in use on the Llandudno branch in 2018. In the steam preservation era the North Wales route, and the section between Llandudno Junction and Llandudno has often been used by steam locomotives hauling charter trains. *Ian Turnbull/Rail Photoprints*

Stanier 'Black Five' BR No 44708 is seen inside the roundhouse shed at Derby in the company of D7542 a Derby built 'Class 25' dating from April 1965 and a partially visible '08' shunter. Note that the lettering TRAFFORD PARK although faded, is still discernible on the locomotive's buffer beam. *Rail Photoprint Collection*

## 44738-44747 June-July, 10 locomotives built at Crewe Works

Introduced with Domed Boilers, Sloping Throatplates and 28 element Superheaters. These locomotives were built with Caprotti single central drive valve gear (poppet valves). Configured with 27ft 6in wheelbase also a change in the coupled wheelbase, 7ft + 8ft to 7ft+ 8ft 4in. (plain bearings). The boiler pitch was set at 2in above standard, and overall height to top of chimney was 2in more than standard (12ft 10in from 12ft 8in). The smokeboxes were constructed to be 4in longer.

They were fitted with low running plates and open-work footsteps. All Ivatt modifications.

### Caprotti Valve Gear

Caprotti valve gear is a distinctively different type of steam locomotive valve gear which was invented and first introduced by Italian engineer Arturo Caprotti. The system uses camshaft and associated poppet valves rather than the various types of piston valves more conventionally used by locomotive designers/builders. The Caprotti system was based on valves used in internal combustion engine design which Caprotti significantly changed to make the method suitable for use with steam engines. In the 1950s the system was further improved and the resulting equipment from that development became known as British Caprotti valve gear. A system of the so called 'inside Caprotti valve gear' was fitted to British Railways built 'Black Fives' Nos 44738–44757.

Stanier 'Black Five' BR No 44739 fitted with inside Caprotti valve gear and then allocated to Llandudno Junction (7A), gets smartly away from Helsby with a Manchester – North Wales service, in the spring of 1949. Note the distinctive front end. The photographer's son has found a good vantage point! *R. A. Whitfield/Rail Photoprints*

This Crewe Works BR built locomotive (Lot 187) entered traffic during June 1948 and was withdrawn from Speke Junction (8C) in January 1965. After a working life of 16 years, 6 months and 12 days it was cut up by Maden & McKee of Stanley, Liverpool during May 1965.

Stanier 'Black Five' BR No 44742 then allocated to Llandudno Junction (7A) gets away from Halton with a North Wales – Manchester service, in the summer of 1949. Note that the pair of mechanical lubricators have been positioned on the right hand running plate between the centre and forward driving wheels. *R. A. Whitfield/Rail Photoprints*

This Crewe Works BR built locomotive (Lot 187) entered traffic during July 1948 and was withdrawn from Southport (27C) in March 1962. After a working life of 15 years, 9 months and 27 days it was cut up by Crewe Works during June 1964.

Stanier 'Black Five' BR No 44744 then allocated to Longsight (9A) is seen when about to take water on the depot, circa 1963. Note the details of the valve gear and cylinder, the open-work footsteps and extended sandbox filler necks. *Rail Photoprints Collection*

This Crewe Works BR built locomotive (Lot 187) entered traffic during July 1948 and was withdrawn from Longsight in November 1963. After a working life of 15 years, 3 months and 28 days it was cut up by Crewe Works during January 1964.

## 44748-44754 February–April, 7 locomotives built at Crewe Works

Introduced with Domed Boilers, Sloping Throatplates and 28 element Superheaters. These locomotives were built with Caprotti single central drive valve gear (poppet valves). Configured with 27ft 6in wheelbase also a change in the coupled wheelbase, 7ft + 8ft to 7ft+ 8ft 4in. (Timken roller bearings) and steel fireboxes.

The boiler pitch was set at 2in above standard, and overall height to top of chimney was 2in more than standard (12ft 10in from 12ft 8in). The smokeboxes were constructed to be 4in longer. They were fitted with low running plates. All Ivatt modifications.

Stanier 'Black Five' BR No 44751 then allocated to Speke Junction (8C) is seen on depot whilst taking water and the fireman is perched on top of the coal with the valve chain in hand, circa 1962. Several distinctive design features of the inside Caprotti variant are shown to good effect in this image. *Mike Stokes Archive*

This Crewe Works BR built locomotive (Lot 187) entered traffic during March 1948 and was withdrawn from Speke Junction in September 1964. After a working life of 16 years, 5 months and 18 days it was cut up by W.E. Smith of Ecclesfield during February 1965.

Stanier 'Black Five' BR No 44753 then allocated to Holbeck (20A) is seen to good effect in this three-quarter front view dating from July 1951. Note that 'Jubilee' class BR No 45597 BARBADOS was also on shed at that time. *Harold Hodgson – Chris Davies Collection/Rail Photoprints*

This Crewe Works BR built locomotive (Lot 187) entered traffic during March 1948 and was withdrawn from Speke Junction in July 1965. After a working life of 17 years, 3 months and 3 days it was cut up by Birds of Long Marston during January 1966.

## 44755-44757 April–December, 3 locomotives built at Crewe Works

Introduced with Domed Boilers, Sloping Throatplates and 28 element Superheaters. These locomotives were built with Caprotti single central drive valve gear (poppet valves). Fitted with double blastpipes and chimneys. Configured with 27ft 6in wheelbase also a change in the coupled wheelbase, 7ft + 8ft to 7ft+ 8ft 4in. (Timken roller bearings). The boiler pitch was set at 2in above standard, and overall height to top of chimney was 2in more than standard (12ft 10in from 12ft 8in). The smokeboxes were constructed to be 4in longer. They were fitted with low running plates. All Ivatt modifications.

Stanier 'Black Five' BR No 44755 with double blastpipe and chimney, and at that time allocated to Holbeck (20A) is seen at Crewe Works circa 1949. Note the steam generator above the cylinder, and also an electric light in front of the double chimney. The locomotive is fitted with a temporary test/indicating shelter. The indicating shelter attached to the front of a locomotive was for members of the engineering staff to ride in for the purpose of taking indicator diagrams of the expansion of the steam in the cylinders and also collecting various items of smoke-box data. *Rail Photoprints Collection*

This Crewe Works BR built locomotive (Lot 187) entered traffic during May 1948 and was withdrawn from Stockport Edgeley (9B) in November 1963. After a working life of 15 years, 5 months and 30 days it was cut up by Crewe Works during February 1964.

Stanier 'Black Five' BR No 44755 with double blastpipe and chimney, and at that time allocated to Holbeck (55A) stands at the buffer stops having arrived at Bath Green Park station with the 08.20 Bristol Temple Meads–Bournemouth West service, 25 July 1959. The locomotive had in all probability worked an earlier Leeds–Bristol service before being unusually rostered to this working. Note the plume of steam at the far end of the train which indicates that the locomotive for the next part of the journey is attached. After being released the 'Black Five' would back down to the shed for servicing and turning. *Hugh Ballantyne/Rail Photoprints*

Stanier 'Black Five' BR No 44755 then allocated to Stockport Edgeley (9B) is seen on shed at Bushbury, on 6 May 1962. Note that the top of the buffer beam is lower than the height of the running plate. Note also the battery box and AWS reservoir cylinder (tank) both located on the running board between the mechanical lubricators and the cab front and also the higher sandbox filler necks. *Ian Turnbull/Rail Photoprints*

Stanier 'Black Five' BR No 44755 is seen stored 'out of use', but in good exterior condition at Stockport Edgeley (9B) in March 1963, just eight months before it was withdrawn. *Rail Photoprints Collection*

# 1949

## 44728-44737 January-March, 10 locomotives built at Crewe Works

Introduced with Domed Boilers, Sloping Throatplates and 28 element Superheaters. British Railways (BR) built locomotives. To simplify frame marking-off and machining the longer 27ft 6in wheelbase also, a change in the coupled wheelbase, 7ft + 8ft to 7ft+ 8ft 4in was adopted as standard for all locomotives in Lot Nos 192 and 199 irrespective of Valve motion and Axlebox bearing types (in this instance plain bearings). The smokeboxes were constructed to be 4in longer (all Ivatt modifications).

This Crewe Works BR built locomotive (Lot 192) entered traffic during January 1949 and was withdrawn from Stockport Edgeley in October 1966. After a working life of 17 years, 7 months and 30 days it was cut up by Drapers of Hull during February 1967.

Stanier 'Black Five' BR No 44729 then allocated to Stockport Edgeley (9B) is seen approaching Moore with the 06.10 Blackpool South–Euston service, on 28 May 1966. *Hugh Ballantyne/ Rail Photoprints*

Stanier 'Black Five' BR No 44730 then allocated to Warrington Dallam (8B) is seen on the curve at Farington Junction circa 1960. *Rail Photoprints Collection*

This Crewe Works BR built locomotive (Lot 192) entered traffic during February 1949 and was withdrawn from Birkenhead Mollington Street (8H) in November 1967. After a working life of 18 years, 8 months and 3 days it was cut up by Cashmores of Great Bridge during March 1968.

Stanier 'Black Five' BR No 44733 then allocated to Carnforth (10A) is seen approaching Mirfield with the 19.15 Wakefield Kirkgate to Preston service, on 1 June 1963. *Ian Turnbull/ Rail Photoprints*

This Crewe Works BR built locomotive (Lot 192) entered traffic during February 1949 and was withdrawn from Carnforth (10A) in June 1967. After a working life of 18 years, 3 months and 3 days it was cut up by Motherwell Machinery & Scrap of Wishaw during November 1967.

https://www.youtube.com/watch?v=5QLxJ0jvV7Q
*44871 & 45407 – Double Headed Black Fives*
*Compilation* – Marsh Steam Videos

https://www.youtube.com/watch?v=foAtqmDpAQ0
*Two Fives Are Better Than One* – Linesider Video

Stanier 'Black Five' BR No 44737 with a Bank Hall (8K) shedplate and its previous shed BOLTON stencilled on the buffer beam, is seen traversing Salwick Troughs (between Preston and Blackpool) with a service for Blackpool, 9 July 1966. *Hugh Ballantyne/Rail Photoprints*

This Crewe Works BR built locomotive (Lot 192) entered traffic during March 1949 and was withdrawn from Springs Branch (8F) in January 1967. After a working life of 17 years and 9 months it was cut up by Cashmores of Newport during July 1967.

## 44718-44727 March–May, 10 locomotives built at Crewe Works

Introduced with Domed Boilers, Sloping Throatplates and 28 element Superheaters. British Railways (BR) built locomotives. To simplify frame marking-off and machining the longer 27ft 6in wheelbase also, a change in the coupled wheelbase, 7ft + 8ft to 7ft+ 8ft 4in was adopted as standard for all locomotives in Lot Nos 192 and 199 irrespective of Valve motion and Axlebox bearing types (in this instance plain bearings). Built with steel fireboxes. The smokeboxes were constructed to be 4in longer (all Ivatt modifications).

Stanier 'Black Five' BR No 44718 then allocated to St. Rollox Shed (65B), is seen passing Robroyston East with an east-bound train of mineral empties on 23 February 1961. *J & J Collection – Sid Rickard/Rail Photoprints*

This Crewe Works BR built locomotive (Lot 192) entered traffic during March 1949 and was withdrawn from Ayr (67C) in November 1966. After a working life of 17 years and 7 months it was cut up by Motherwell Machinery & Scrap of Wishaw during April 1967 having been allocated to Scottish depots for the whole of the BR era.

Stanier 'Black Five' BR No 44720 then allocated to Perth South (63A) pilots ex GCR 'D11' Large Director 4-4-0 BR No 62691 LAIRD of BALMAWHAPPLE south-bound off Jamestown Viaduct and towards the Forth Bridge on 23 June 1956. The Jamestown Viaduct is part of the northern approach to the Forth Bridge. It crosses the hamlet of Jamestown and the village of North Queensferry in Fife. It spans the B981 public road and the former branch railway to North Queensferry, and Rosyth for the famous naval dockyard. The 'D11' looks to have steam to spare! *David Anderson*

This Crewe Works BR built locomotive (Lot 192) entered traffic during March 1949 and was withdrawn from Dundee Tay Bridge (62B) in October 1966. After a working life of 17 years, 5 months and 30 days it was cut up by Arnott Young of Old Kilpatrick during June 1967 having been allocated to Scottish depots for the whole of the BR era.

Stanier 'Black Five' BR No 44721 then allocated to Perth South (63A) is seen after crossing Jamestown Viaduct with a Perth to Edinburgh Waverley service, circa July 1957. Note that a member of the footplate crew was intent on being in the picture. *David Anderson*

This Crewe Works BR built locomotive (Lot 192) entered traffic during March 1949 and was withdrawn from Polmadie (66A) in July 1965. After a working life of 16 years, 2 months and 30 days it was cut up by Motherwell Machinery & Scrap of Wishaw during November 1965.

Stanier 'Black Five' BR No 44724 then allocated to Inverness (60A) is seen at its home shed, circa 1956. *Rail Photoprints Collection*

This Crewe Works BR built locomotive (Lot 192) entered traffic during April 1949 and was withdrawn from Ayr (67C) in October 1966. After a working life of 17 years and 5 months it was cut up by Motherwell Machinery & Scrap of Wishaw during January 1967, having been allocated to Scottish depots for the whole of the BR era.

Stanier 'Black Five' BR No 44725 then allocated to Speke Junction (8C) is seen on Dillicar Troughs with a south-bound freight during March 1964. *Rail Photoprints Collection*

This Crewe Works BR built locomotive (Lot 192) entered traffic during April 1949 and was withdrawn from Speke Junction in October 1967. After a working life of 18 years and 5 months it was cut up by Cashmores of Great Bridge during March 1968.

## 44658-44667 May–July, 10 locomotives built at Crewe Works

Introduced with Domed Boilers, Sloping Throatplates and 28 element Superheaters. British Railways (BR) built locomotives. To simplify frame marking-off and machining the longer 27ft 6in wheelbase also, a change in the coupled wheelbase, 7ft + 8ft to 7ft+ 8ft 4in was adopted as standard for all locomotives in Lot Nos 192 and 199 irrespective of Valve motion and Axlebox bearing types (in this instance plain bearings). The smokeboxes were constructed to be 4in longer (all Ivatt modifications). This batch of 10 locomotives became the first in the BR 'Black Five' class numbering system.

Stanier 'Black Five' BR No 44664 then allocated to Derby (17A) is seen piloting an unidentified re-built 'Royal Scot' near New Mills, with a down express during August 1962. *Alan H. Bryant ARPS/Rail Photoprints*

This Crewe Works BR built locomotive (Lot 199) entered traffic during July 1949 and was withdrawn from Bolton (9K) in September 1968. After a working life of 18 years, 9 months and 14 days it was cut up by Drapers of Hull during September 1968.

Stanier 'Black Five' BR No 44664 with a Preston (10B) shedplate is seen ex works at Crewe in the company of 'Britannia' class BR No 70009 ALFRED THE GREAT and an unidentified 'Black Five' locomotive, all were waiting to be returned to service during May 1965. Note the diesel locomotives in the background. *Colin Whitfield/Rail Photoprints*

Stanier 'Black Five' BR No 44665 then allocated to Colwick (16B) is seen departing Marylebone station with a down GC route service for Nottingham, circa 1965. *John Day Collection/Rail Photoprints*

Stanier 'Black Five' BR No 44666 then allocated to Saltley (21A) is seen waiting to depart Marylebone station with a GC route service for Nottingham in June 1965. *Keith Langston Collection*

This Crewe Works BR built locomotive (Lot 199) entered traffic during July 1949 and was withdrawn from Trafford Park (9E) in March 1968. After a working life of 18 years, 7 months and 13 days it was cut up by Drapers of Hull during June 1968.

This Crewe Works BR built locomotive (Lot 199) entered traffic during July 1949 and was withdrawn from Edge Hill (8A) in February 1967. After a working life of 17 years, 6 months and 15 days it was cut up by Drapers of Hull during September 1967.

Stanier 'Black Five' BR No 44667 then allocated to Carnforth(10A) and piloting an unidentified 'Jubilee' class locomotive is seen approaching Disley Tunnel with a down express for Manchester, circa 1966. *Alan H. Bryant ARPS/Rail Photoprints*

This Crewe Works BR built locomotive (Lot 199) entered traffic during July 1949 and was withdrawn from Carnforth in September 1967. After a working life of 18 years it was cut up by Drapers of Hull during September 1967.

## 44668-44669 December, 2 locomotives built at Horwich Works

Introduced with Domed Boilers, Sloping Throatplates and 28 element Superheaters. Boilers built at Crewe. British Railways (BR) built locomotives. To simplify frame marking-off and machining the longer 27ft 6in wheelbase also, a change in the coupled wheelbase, 7ft + 8ft to 7ft+ 8ft 4in was adopted as standard for all locomotives in Lot Nos 192 and 199 irrespective of Valve motion and Axlebox bearing types (Skefko roller bearings on the driving coupled axle only). The smokeboxes were constructed to be 4in longer (all Ivatt modifications).

Stanier 'Black Five' BR No 44668 then allocated to Carlisle Kingmoor (12A) is seen shunting at Carstairs Junction during September 1956. Note this locomotive was only ever allocated to Carlisle Kingmoor but carried the earlier (68A) Carlisle Kingmoor shed code until the Spring of 1958. *David Anderson*

This Horwich Works BR built locomotive (Lot 199) entered traffic during December 1949 and was withdrawn from Carlisle Kingmoor in April 1966. After a working life of 16 years, 3 months and 7 days it was cut up by Motherwell Machinery & Scrap during July 1966.

Stanier 'Black Five' BR No 44668 is seen hard at work with an up fitted train of vans on a straight section of track near Symington on the West Coast Main Line (WCML) during April 1960. *David Anderson*

# 1950

## 44670-44677 January-April, 8 locomotives built at Horwich Works

Introduced with Domed Boilers, Sloping Throatplates and 28 element Superheaters. British Railways (BR) built locomotives. To simplify frame marking-off and machining the longer 27ft 6in wheelbase also, a change in the coupled wheelbase 7ft + 8ft to 7ft+ 8ft 4in was adopted as standard for all locomotives in Lot Nos 192 and 199 irrespective of Valve motion and Axlebox bearing types (in this instance Skefko roller bearings on the driving coupled axle). The smokeboxes were constructed to be 4in longer (all Ivatt modifications). Boilers built at Crewe.

Stanier 'Black Five' BR No 44671 then allocated to Carlisle Kingmoor (68A) is seen at Crawford whilst working 'wrong line' with a West Coast Main Line freight, on Sunday 19 April 1959. Note that the top feed is located on the forward ring of the boiler barrel. *David Anderson*

This Horwich Works BR built locomotive (Lot 199) entered traffic during February 1950 and was withdrawn from Carlisle Kingmoor (then 12A) in February 1967. After a working life of 16 years, 11 months and 3 days it was cut up by J. McWilliams of Shettleston during June 1967.

Stanier 'Black Five' BR No 44673 then allocated to Lostock Hall (10D) is seen with an up train at Beattock Summit during July 1959. Note the buffer stops at the head of the relief/refuge siding to the right of the locomotive and the signal box in the background. In this instance the locomotive's top feed is located on the second (middle) section of the boiler barrel. The gradient marker on the embankment to the right indicates the forthcoming falling incline section of track. *David Anderson*

This Horwich Works BR built locomotive (Lot 199) entered traffic during February 1950 and was withdrawn from Trafford Park (9E) in May 1965. After a working life of 15 years, 2 months and 2 days it was cut up by Crewe Works during August 1965.

Stanier 'Black Five' BR No 44676 then allocated to Carlisle Kingmoor (12A) is seen in the company of sister locomotive BR No 44993 (built Horwich 1947). The pair were heading down to Edinburgh Princess Street station, from Edinburgh Dalry Road shed in order to work the returning Royal Train to London Euston via the WCML on 22 June 1960. *David Anderson*

This Horwich Works BR built locomotive (Lot 199) entered traffic during April 1950 and was withdrawn from Newton Heath (9D) in July 1964. After a working life of 14 years and 2 months it was cut up by Crewe Works during July 1964.

The Royal Train is seen passing Kingsnowe west of Edinburgh with BR No 44676 piloting BR No 44993. Note the 4-lamp headcode. Both images. *David Anderson*

Stanier 'Black Five' BR No 44677 then allocated to Carlisle Kingmoor (12A) is seen passing Gretna Junction signal box heading north with a fitted freight during June 1964. Note the self-weighing tender. *Rail Photoprints Collection*

This Horwich Works BR built locomotive (Lot 199) entered traffic during April 1950 and was withdrawn from Carlisle Kingmoor in October 1967. After a working life of 17 years and 5 months it was cut up by J. McWilliams of Shettleston during April 1968.

## 44678-44685 May-August, 8 locomotives built at Horwich Works

Introduced with Domed Boilers, Sloping Throatplates and 28 element Superheaters. British Railways (BR) built locomotives.

To simplify frame marking-off and machining the longer 27ft 6in wheelbase, also a change in the coupled wheelbase, 7ft + 8ft to 7ft+ 8ft 4in. was adopted as standard for all locomotives in Lot Nos 192 and 199 irrespective of Valve motion and Axlebox bearing types (in this instance Skefko roller bearings throughout). The smokeboxes were constructed to be 4in longer (all Ivatt modifications). Boilers built at Crewe.

Stanier 'Black Five' BR No 44680 then allocated to Crewe South (5B) is seen whilst climbing the final yards to Shap Summit with a down Saturday extra, on 15 July 1967. *Chris Davies/ Rail Photoprints*

This Horwich Works BR built locomotive (Lot 199) entered traffic during June 1950 and was withdrawn from Crewe South in September 1967. After a working life of 17 years, 2 months and 1 day it was cut up by Cohens of Kettering during March 1968.

Stanier 'Black Five' BR No 44681 then allocated to Crewe North (5A) is seen near Dunham Hill with a Llandudno–Manchester service, during August 1951. *R. A. Whitfield/Rail Photoprints*

This Horwich Works BR built locomotive (Lot 199) entered traffic during June 1950 and was withdrawn from Crewe South (5B) in September 1967. After a working life of 17 years, 2 months and 14 days it was cut up by Cohens of Kettering during March 1968.

## 44688–44697 May–August, 10 locomotives built at Horwich Works

Introduced with Domed Boilers, Sloping Throatplates and 28 element Superheaters. British Railways (BR) built locomotives. To simplify frame marking-off and machining the longer 27ft 6in wheelbase

Also, a change in the coupled wheelbase, 7ft + 8ft to 7ft+ 8ft 4in was adopted as standard for all locomotives in Lot Nos 192 and 199 irrespective of Valve motion and Axlebox bearing types (in this instance Timken roller bearings on driving coupled axle). The smokeboxes were constructed to be 4in longer (all Ivatt modifications). Boilers built at Crewe.

The end of BR steam – Rose Grove (10F) motive power depot in August 1968 with Stanier 'Black Five' BR No 44690 then allocated to Rose Grove and seen in the company of sister Rose Grove engine BR No 44899 (Crewe built 1945). Note 'Steam Forever' chalked on the tender of the Crewe built engine and the piles of coal removed from the tenders. The breakers torch awaits! *Gordon Edgar Collection/Rail Photoprints*

This Horwich Works BR built locomotive (Lot 199) entered traffic during October 1950 and was withdrawn from Rose Grove in August 1968. After a working life of 17 years and 9 months it was cut up by J. McWilliams of Shettleston during September 1968.

Stanier 'Black Five' BR No 44691 then allocated to Leicester (15E) is seen arriving at Nottingham Victoria with the 09.30 Sheffield–Swindon inter-regional service, on 18 June 1960.
*Hugh Ballantyne/Rail Photoprints*

This Horwich Works BR built locomotive (Lot 199) entered traffic during October 1950 and was withdrawn from Workington (12D) in April 1967. After a working life of 17 years and 5 months it was cut up by Campbells of Airdrie during December 1967.

Bedford allocated (14E) Stanier 'Black Five' BR No 44691, awaits instruction at Olney station as it heads a very short pick up freight on the Northampton-Bedford line, during March 1962. Note the shunter having a conversation with the guard. *A. J. B. Dodd/Rail Photoprints*

Stanier 'Black Five' BR No 44697 was paired with a self-weighing tender when seen at Newton Heath (9D), circa 1965. Note that the shed plate had been removed with the code being stencilled onto the firebox door. *Rail Photoprints Collection*

This Horwich Works BR built locomotive (Lot 199) entered traffic during November 1950 and was withdrawn from Newton Heath in November 1967. After a working life of 16 years, 11 months and 1 day it was cut up by Cashmores of Great Bridge during April 1968.

# 1951

## 44686-44687 April–May, 2 locomotives built at Horwich Works

Introduced with Domed Boilers, Sloping Throatplates and 28 element Superheaters. British Railways (BR) built locomotives. To simplify frame marking-off and machining the longer 27ft 6in wheelbase also, a change in the coupled wheelbase, 7ft + 8ft to 7ft+ 8ft 4in was adopted as standard for all locomotives in Lot Nos 192 and 199 irrespective of Valve motion and Axlebox bearing types (in this instance Skefko roller bearings on all axles).

These were the last two locomotives of the class to be built. They were fitted with outside Caprotti valve gear and very high running plates in accordance with the BR Standard practice. Both locomotives were fitted with double blastpipes and chimneys.

The smokeboxes were constructed to be 4in longer (all Ivatt modifications). Boilers built at Crewe.

Caprotti 'Black Five' BR No 44686 is seen at Southport (27C) in August 1964. Note the outside drive revised Caprotti motion, double chimney, high running plate and open work footsteps.
*Norman Preedy*

This Horwich Works BR built locomotive (Lot 199) entered traffic during April 1951 and was withdrawn from Southport in October 1965. After a working life of 14 years and 5 months it was cut up by T. W. Ward of Sheffield during September 1967.

Caprotti 'Black Five' BR No 44686 then allocated to Llandudno Junction (6G) is seen passing through Salford on a very gloomy day as it leaves Manchester with a North Wales Coast service, circa April 1962. *Jim Carter Rail Photoprints*

https://www.youtube.com/watch?v=WsaeDbUjX8c
*Vintage Rail Film: Engine Shed 1938 LMS –*
The Steam Channel

Caprotti 'Black Five' BR No 44687, the last Stanier 'Black Five' to be built and then allocated to Llandudno Junction (6G) takes a spin on the Patricroft turntable, during September 1960. In addition to the main distinctive features note also that the righthand side running plate was constructed in two sections in order to accommodate the mechanical lubricators. *Jim Carter/Rail Photoprints*

This Horwich Works BR built locomotive (Lot 199) entered traffic during May 1951 and was withdrawn from Southport (8M) in January 1966. After a working life of 14 years and 7 months it was cut up by Cashmores of Great Bridge during March 1966.

For some time, there has been the formulation of plans to create a new build rolling chassis for a British Caprotti 'Black Five' and in that regard a new fund has been set up entitled 'Caprotti Black 5 Fund' (formerly Caprotti Black 5 Limited). To date drawings have been obtained and initial research work undertaken. For more information visit www.britishcaprottiblack5.org.uk

# Tender Numbers

| LMS/BR Running numbers | Tenders number (Initial attachment) |
|---|---|
| 5000–5019 | 9002/54–64/7–72, 9164/5 Crw |
| 5020–5069 | 9074–9123 VF |
| 5070–5074 | 9166–8, 9000/1 Crw |
| 5075–5124 | 9169–9218 VF |
| 5125–5224 | 9229–9328 AW |
| 5225–5451 | 9641–9687 AW |
| 5452–5461 | 9708–9717 Crw Above. |
| 5462–5471 | 9718–9727 Crw |
| 5472–5481 | 9818–9827 Der |
| 5482–5496 | 9828–9842 Der |
| 5497–5499, 4800–4806 | 9843–9852 Der |
| 4807–4825 | 10432–10450 Der |
| 4826–4835 | 10451–10460 Crw |
| 4836–4845 | 10461–10470 Crw |
| 4846–4855 | 10471–10480 Crw File 45225 |
| 4856–4865 | 10481–10490 Crw |
| 4866–4871 | 10491–10496 Crw |
| 4872–4891 | 10497–10516 Crw |
| 4892–4911 | 10517– 10536 Crw |
| 4912–4931 | 10537–10556 Crw |
| 4932–4941 | 10557–10566 Hor |
| 4942–4966 | 10567–10589, 10611, 10591 Hor |
| 4967–4981 | 10592–10606 Crw |
| 4982–4996 | 10607–10610, 10590, 10612–10621 Hor |
| 4997–4999, 4783–4789 | 10670–10679 Hor |
| 4790–4799 | 10680–10689 Hor |
| 4768–4782 | 10625–10639 Crw |
| 4758–4767 | 10640–10649 Crw |
| 4748–4757 | 10650–10659 Crw |
| 44738–44747 | 10660–10669 Crw |
| 44698–44717 | 10690–10709 Hor |
| 44718–44737 | 10710–10729 Crw |
| 44658–44667 | 10798–10807 Crw |
| 44668–44697 | 10808–10816, 10837, 10818–10836, 10817 Hor |

LMS rivetted tender. *Mike Morant Collection*

LMS Welded tender. *Mike Morant Collection*

BR Welded tender, lined out. *Rail Photoprints Collection*

A Self weighing tender attached to Stanier 'Black Five' BR No 44697, seen on the turntable at Newton Heath. Early BR logo, lined. *Rail Photoprints Collection*

BR Welded tender, later logo 1956 onwards. *David Anderson*

BR rivetted tender, early logo 1950-56, fully lined out. *Rail Photoprints Collection*

# BR Shed Codes

## BR 1948 – LMR

| | |
|---|---|
| 1A | Willesden |
| 1B | Camden |
| 1C | Watford |
| 1D | Devons Road |
| | |
| 2A | Rugby |
| 2B | Nuneaton |
| 2C | Warwick |
| 2D | Coventry |
| | |
| 3A | Bescot |
| 3B | Bushbury |
| 3C | Walsall |
| 3D | Aston |
| 3E | Monument Lane |
| | |
| 4A | Bletchley |
| 4B | Northampton |
| | |
| 5A | Crewe North |
| 5B | Crewe South |
| 5C | Stafford |
| 5D | Stoke |
| 5E | Alsager |
| 5F | Uttoxeter |
| | |
| 6A | Chester |
| 6B | Mold Junction |
| 6C | Birkenhead |
| 6D | Northgate |
| 6E | Wrexham |
| 6F | Bidston |
| | |
| 7A | Llandudno Junction |
| 7B | Bangor |
| 7C | Holyhead |
| 7D | Rhyl |
| | |
| 8A | Edge Hill |
| 8B | Warrington (Dallam) |
| 8C | Speke Junction |
| 8D | Widnes |
| 8E | Brunswick |
| 8E | Warrington |

| | |
|---|---|
| 9A | Longsight |
| 9B | Stockport Edgeley |
| 9C | Macclesfield |
| 9D | Buxton |
| 9E | Trafford Park |
| 9F | Heaton Mersey |
| 9G | Northwich |
| | |
| 10A | Springs Branch (Wigan) |
| 10B | Preston |
| 10C | Patricroft |
| 10D | Plodder Lane |
| 10E | Sutton Oak |
| 10F | Wigan (Lower Ince) |
| | |
| 11A | Carnforth |
| 11B | Barrow |
| 11C | Oxenholme |
| 11D | Tebay |
| | |
| 12A | Carlisle (Upperby) |
| 12B | Carlisle (Canal) |
| 12C | Penrith |
| 12D | Workington |
| 12E | Moor Row |
| | |
| 14A | Cricklewood |
| 14B | Kentish Town |
| 14C | St. Albans |
| | |
| 15A | Wellingborough |
| 15B | Kettering |
| 15C | Leicester |
| 15D | Bedford |
| | |
| 16A | Nottingham |
| 16C | Kirkby |
| 16D | Mansfield |
| | |
| 17A | Derby |
| 17B | Burton |
| 17C | Coalville |
| 17D | Rowsley |
| | |
| 18A | Toton |
| 18B | Westhouses |

| | |
|---|---|
| 18C | Hasland |
| 18D | Staveley |
| | |
| 19A | Sheffield |
| 19B | Millhouses |
| 19C | Canklow |
| | |
| 20A | Leeds |
| 20B | Stourton |
| 20C | Royston |
| 20D | Normanton |
| 20E | Manningham |
| | |
| 21A | Saltley |
| 21B | Bournville |
| 21C | Bromsgrove |
| 21D | Stratford-on-Avon |
| | |
| 22A | Bristol |
| 22B | Gloucester |
| | |
| 23A | Skipton |
| 23B | Hellifield |
| 23C | Lancaster |
| | |
| 24A | Accrington |
| 24B | Rose Grove |
| 24C | Lostock Hall |
| 24D | Lower Darwen |
| | |
| 25A | Wakefield |
| 25B | Huddersfield |
| 25C | Goole |
| 25D | Mirfield |
| 25E | Sowerby Bridge |
| 25F | Low Moor |
| 25G | Farnley Junction |
| | |
| 26A | Newton Heath |
| 26B | Agecroft |
| 26C | Bolton |
| 26D | Bury |
| 26E | Bacup |
| 26F | Lees |
| 26G | Belle Vue |

27A  Bank Hall
27B  Aintree
27C  Southport
27D  Wigan (Central L&Y)
27E  Walton
27E  Southport

28A  Blackpool
28B  Fleetwood

**BR 1948 – ER**
30A  Stratford
30B  Hertford East
30C  Bishops Stortford
30D  Southend Victoria
30E  Colchester
30F  Parkeston

31A  Cambridge
31B  March
31C  King's Lynn
31D  South Lynn
31E  Bury St. Edmunds

32A  Norwich
32B  Ipswich
32C  Lowestoft
32D  Yarmouth (South Town)
32E  Yarmouth (Vauxhall)
32F  Yarmouth Beach
32G  Melton Constable

33A  Plaistow
33B  Tilbury
33C  Shoeburyness

34A  Kings Cross
34B  Hornsey
34C  Hatfield
34D  Hitchen
34E  Neasden

35A  New England
35B  Grantham
35C  Peterborough (ex L.M.)

36A  Doncaster
36B  Mexborough

36C  Frodingham
36D  Barnsley
36E  Retford

37A  Ardsley
37B  Copley Hill
37C  Bradford

38A  Colwick
38B  Annesley
38C  Leicester
38D  Staveley
38E  Woodford Halse

39A  Gorton
39B  Sheffield

40A  Lincoln
40B  Immingham
40C  Louth
40D  Tuxford
40E  Langwith
40F  Boston

**BR 1948 – NER**
50A  York
50B  Leeds (Neville Hill)
50C  Selby
50D  Starbeck
50E  Scarborough
50F  Malton
50G  Whitby

51A  Darlington
51B  Newport
51C  West Hartlepool
51D  Middlesbrough
51E  Stockton
51F  West Auckland
51G  Haverton Hill
51H  Kirkby Stephen
51J  Northallerton
51K  Saltburn

52A  Gateshead
52B  Heaton
52C  Blaydon
52D  Tweedmouth

52E  Percy Main
52F  North Blyth

53A  Hull (Dairycoates)
53B  Hull (Botanic Gardens)
53C  Hull (Springhead)
53D  Bridlington
53E  Cudworth

54A  Sunderland
54B  Tyne Dock
54C  Borough Gardens
54D  Consett

**BR 1948 – NER ScR**
60A  Inverness
60B  Aviemore
60C  Helmsdale
60D  Wick
60E  Forres

61A  Kittybrewster
61B  Ferryhill
61C  Keith

62A  Thornton
62B  Dundee
62C  Dunfermline

63A  Perth
63B  Stirling
63C  Forfar
63D  Fort William
63E  Oban

64A  St. Margarets
64B  Haymarket
64C  Dalry Road
64D  Carstairs
64E  Polmont
64F  Bathgate
64G  Hawick

65A  Eastfield
65B  St. Rollox
65C  Parkhead
65D  Dawsholme
65E  Kipps

65F  Grangemouth
65G  Yoker
65H  Helensburgh
65I  Balloch

66A  Polmadie
66B  Motherwell
66C  Hamilton
66D  Greenock

67A  Corkerhill
67B  Hurlford
67C  Ayr
67D  Ardrossan

68A  Carlisle Kingmoor
68B  Dumfries
68C  Stranraer
68D  Beattock

**BR 1948 – SR**
70A  Nine Elms
70B  Feltham
70C  Guildford
70D  Basingstoke
70E  Reading

71A  Eastleigh
71B  Bournemouth
71C  Dorchester
71D  Fratton
71G  Bath
71H  Templecombe
71I  Southampton

72A  Exmouth Junction
72B  Salisbury
72C  Yeovil
72D  Plymouth
72E  Barnstable
72F  Wadebridge

73A  Stewarts Lane
73B  Bricklayers Arms

73C  Hither Green
73D  Gillingham
73E  Faversham
74A  Ashford
74B  Ramsgate
74C  Dover
74D  Tonbridge
74E  St. Leonards

75A  Brighton
75B  Redhill
75C  Norwood
75D  Horsham
75E  Three Bridges
75F  Tunbridge Wells
75G  Eastbourne

**BR 1948 – WR**
81A  Old Oak Common
81B  Slough
81C  Southall
81D  Reading
81E  Didcot
81F  Oxford

82A  Bristol (Bath Road)
82B  Bristol (St. Phillips Marsh)
82C  Swindon
82D  Westbury
82E  Yeovil
82F  Weymouth

83A  Newton Abbot
83B  Taunton
83C  Exeter
83D  Laira
83E  St. Blazey
83F  Truro
83G  Penzance

84A  Wolverhampton (Stafford Road)
84B  Oxley
84C  Banbury
84D  Leamington

84E  Tyseley
84F  Stourbridge
84G  Shrewsbury
84H  Wellington
84J  Croes Newydd
84K  Chester
85A  Worcester
85B  Gloucester
85C  Hereford
85D  Kidderminster

86A  Newport (Ebbw Junction)
86B  Newport Pill
86C  Cardiff (Canton)
86D  Llantrisant
86E  Severn Tunnel Junction
86F  Tondu
86G  Pontypool Road
86H  Aberbeeg
86G  Aberdare
86K  Abergavenny

87A  Neath
87B  Duffryn Yard
87C  Danygraig
87D  Swansea East Dock
87E  Landore
87F  Llanelly
87G  Carmarthen
87H  Newland
87J  Goodwick
87K  Swansea Victoria

88A  Cardiff Cathays
88B  Cardiff East Dock
88C  Barry
88D  Merthyr
88E  Abercynon
88F  Treherbert

89A  Oswestry
89B  Brecon
89C  Machynlleth

**Key to Appendix – Locomotives**
(c)  Caprotti inside valve gear.
(C)  Caprotti outside valve gear.
(d)  Double chimney.
(f)  Steel firebox.
(o)  Temporarily converted for oil burning in 1947, later converted back.
(r)  Skefko roller bearings.
(R)  Skefko roller bearings on driving coupled axle only.
(s)  Outside Stephenson valve gear.
(t)  Timken roller bearings.
(T)  Timken roller bearings on driving coupled axle only.
(P)  Preserved locomotive

Stanier 'Black Five' BR No 45194 (an Armstrong Whitworth 1935 built locomotive) passes Ayr Harbour Junction with coal trucks for Ayr Harbour, on 23 June 1961. J & J Collection. *Sid Rickard/Rail Photoprints*

## Appendix - Locomotives 44658-44747 (Shed codes shown are BR 01/01/1948)

| Number BR | LMSR | Built Date/Works | Last Shed/Withdrawn | |
|---|---|---|---|---|
| 44658 | | 05/49 Crw | 10A | 11/67 |
| 44659 | | 05/49 Crw | 27B | 06/67 |
| 44660 | | 05/49 Crw | 21A | 09/64 |
| 44661 | | 06/49 Crw | 5D | 08/67 |
| 44662 | | 06/49 Crw | 25F | 10/67 |
| 44663 | | 06/49 Crw | 13C | 05/68 |
| 44664 | | 06/49 Crw | 26C | 05/68 |
| 44665 | | 06/49 Crw | 13A | 03/68 |
| 44666 | | 07/49 Crw | 8A | 02/67 |
| 44667 | | 07/49 Crw | 11A | 08/67 |
| 44668 R | | 12/49 Hor | 68A | 04/66 |
| 44669 R | | 12/49 Hor | 68A | 10/67 |
| 44670 R | | 01/50 Hor | 68A | 01/66 |
| 44671 R | | 02/50 Hor | 68A | 02/67 |
| 44672 R | | 02/50 Hor | 24C | 03/68 |
| 44673 R | | 02/50 Hor | 13A | 05/65 |
| 44674 R | | 03/50 Hor | 68A | 12/67 |
| 44675 R | | 03/50 Hor | 68A | 09/67 |
| 44676 R | | 04/50 Hor | 26A | 07/64 |
| 44677 R | | 04/50 Hor | 68A | 10/67 |
| 44678 r | | 05/50 Hor | 10A | 11/67 |
| 44679 r | | 05/50 Hor | 10A | 09/67 |
| 44680 r | | 06/50 Hor | 5B | 09/67 |
| 44681 r | | 06/50 Hor | 5B | 09/67 |
| 44682 r | | 06/50 Hor | 10A | 11/67 |
| 44683 r | | 07/50 Hor | 24C | 04/68 |
| 44684 r | | 07/50 Hor | 5B | 09/67 |
| 44685 r | | 08/50 Hor | 5B | 04/67 |
| 44686 Crd | | 04/51 Hor | 13E | 10/65 |
| 44687 Crd | | 05/51 Hor | 13E | 01/66 |
| 44688 T | | 08/50 Hor | 8A | 08/66 |
| 44689 T | | 09/50 Hor | 68A | 03/67 |
| 44690 T | | 10/50 Hor | 24B | 08/68 |
| 44691 T | | 10/50 Hor | 12D | 04/67 |
| 44692 T | | 10/50 Hor | 68A | 05/66 |
| 44693 T | | 11/50 Hor | 25F | 05/67 |
| 44694 T | | 11/50 Hor | 25F | 10/67 |
| 44695 T | | 11/50 Hor | 25F | 06/67 |
| 44696 T | | 11/50 Hor | 26A | 05/67 |
| 44697 T | | 11/50 Hor | 26A | 11/67 |
| 44698 | | 07/48 Hor | 63A | 07/66 |
| 44699 | | 07/48 Hor | 67A | 05/67 |
| 44700 | | 07/48 Hor | 64D | 07/66 |
| 44701 | | 08/48 Hor | 64D | 05/64 |
| 44702 | | 08/48 Hor | 64C | 06/65 |
| 44703 | | 08/48 Hor | 65A | 12/66 |
| 44704 | | 09/48 Hor | 63A | 09/66 |
| 44705 | | 09/48 Hor | 63A | 09/66 |
| 44706 | | 09/48 Hor | 67A | 12/63 |
| 44707 | | 09/48 Hor | 64D | 01/66 |
| 44708 | | 10/48 Hor | 13A | 01/68 |
| 44709 | | 10/48 Hor | 11A | 08/68 |
| 44710 | | 10/48 Hor | 10A | 12/66 |
| 44711 | | 10/48 Hor | 8A | 05/68 |
| 44712 | | 10/48 Hor | 7C | 11/66 |
| 44713 | | 11/48 Hor | 24C | 08/68 |
| 44714 | | 11/48 Hor | 5D | 11/66 |
| 44715 | | 11/48 Hor | 13A | 01/68 |
| 44716 | | 11/48 Hor | 5B | 07/65 |
| 44717 | | 12/48 Hor | 8A | 08/67 |
| 44718 f | | 03/49 Crw | 67C | 11/66 |
| 44719 f | | 03/49 Crw | 65F | 10/64 |
| 44720 f | | 03/49 Crw | 62B | 10/66 |
| 44721 f | | 03/49 Crw | 66A | 07/65 |
| 44722 f | | 04/49 Crw | 63A | 04/67 |
| 44723 f | | 04/49 Crw | 67A | 10/66 |
| 44724 f | | 04/49 Crw | 67C | 10/66 |
| 44725 f | | 04/49 Crw | 8C | 10/67 |
| 44726 f | | 05/49 Crw | 68A | 10/66 |
| 44727 f | | 05/49 Crw | 68A | 10/67 |
| 44728 | | 01/49 Crw | 26C | 01/68 |
| 44729 | | 01/49 Crw | 9B | 10/66 |
| 44730 | | 02/49 Crw | 6C | 11/67 |
| 44731 | | 02/49 Crw | 8B | 05/66 |
| 44732 | | 02/49 Crw | 10A | 07/67 |
| 44733 | | 02/49 Crw | 11A | 06/67 |
| 44734 | | 02/49 Crw | 26A | 12/67 |
| 44735 | | 02/49 Crw | 11A | 08/68 |
| 44736 | | 02/49 Crw | 26A | 09/67 |
| 44737 | | 03/49 Crw | 10A | 01/67 |
| 44738 c | | 06/48 Crw | 8C | 06/64 |
| 44739 c | | 06/48 Crw | 8C | 01/65 |
| 44740 c | | 05/48 Crw | 7A | 04/63 |
| 44741 c | | 06/48 Crw | 8C | 03/65 |
| 44742 c | | 07/48 Crw | 13E | 05/64 |
| 44743 c | | 06/48 Crw | 8C | 01/66 |
| 44744 c | | 07/48 Crw | 9A | 11/63 |
| 44745 c | | 07/48 Crw | 13E | 10/64 |
| 44746 c | | 08/48 Crw | 26C | 02/64 |
| 44747 c | | 07/48 Crw | 9A | 04/63 |

## Appendix - Locomotives 44748-44837

| Number BR | LMSR | Built Date/Works | Last Shed/ Withdrawn | | Number BR | LMSR | Built Date/Works | Last Shed/ Withdrawn | |
|---|---|---|---|---|---|---|---|---|---|
| 44748 | M4748 ct | 02/48 Crw | 9A | 09/64 | 44793 | 4793 | 08/47 Hor | 63A | 12/64 |
| 44749 | M4749 ct | 02/48 Crw | 8C | 09/64 | 44794 | 4794 | 08/47 Hor | 63A | 04/67 |
| 44750 | M4750 ct | 02/48 Crw | 8C | 09/63 | 44795 | 4795 | 08/47 Hor | 68A | 07/67 |
| 44751 | M4751 ct | 03/48 Crw | 8C | 09/64 | 44796 | 4796 | 09/47 Hor | 66A | 05/67 |
| 44752 | M4752 ct | 03/48 Crw | 9B | 04/64 | 44797 | 4797 | 09/47 Hor | 63A | 09/66 |
| 44753 | M4753 ct | 03/48 Crw | 8C | 07/65 | 44798 | 4798 | 10/47 Hor | 67A | 09/66 |
| 44754 ct | | 04/48 Crw | 8C | 04/64 | 44799 | 4799 | 10/47 Hor | 63A | 07/65 |
| 44755 ctd | | 05/48 Crw | 9B | 11/63 | 44800 | 4800 | 05/44 Der | 24C | 03/68 |
| 44756 ctd | | 06/48 Crw | 13E | 09/64 | 44801 | 4801 | 05/44 Der | 67B | 05/64 |
| 44757 ctd | | 12/48 Crw | 13E | 11/65 | 44802 | 4802 | 06/44 Der | 26C | 06/68 |
| 44758 | 4758 t | 09/47 Crw | 11A | 07/68 | 44803 | 4803 | 06/44 Der | 26A | 06/68 |
| 44759 | 4759 t | 09/47 Crw | 68A | 11/67 | 44804 | 4804 | 06/44 Der | 13A | 03/68 |
| 44760 | 4760 t | 09/47 Crw | 5D | 10/66 | 44805 | 4805 | 06/44 Der | 5B | 09/67 |
| 44761 | 4761 t | 10/47 Crw | 24C | 04/68 | 44806 | 4806 P | 07/44 Der | 24C | 08/68 |
| 44762 | 4762 t | 10/47 Crw | 84J | 11/66 | 44807 | 4807 | 09/44 Der | 13A | 03/68 |
| 44763 | 4763 t | 10/47 Crw | 1A | 09/65 | 44808 | 4808 | 09/44 Der | 84B | 12/66 |
| 44764 | 4764 t | 11/47 Crw | 6B | 09/65 | 44809 | 4809 | 09/44 Der | 11A | 08/68 |
| 44765 | 4765 td | 12/47 Crw | 5B | 09/67 | 44810 | 4810 | 10/44 Der | 5D | 08/66 |
| 44766 | 4766 td | 12/47 Crw | 5B | 08/67 | 44811 | 4811 | 10/44 Der | 38A | 10/66 |
| 44767 | 4767 tdsP | 12/47 Crw | 68A | 12/67 | 44812 | 4812 | 10/44 Der | 5B | 09/67 |
| 44768 | 4768 | 04/47 Crw | 8A | 06/67 | 44813 | 4813 | 10/44 Der | 5D | 09/66 |
| 44769 | 4769 | 04/47 Crw | 65A | 07/65 | 44814 | 4814 | 10/44 Der | 5B | 09/67 |
| 44770 | 4770 | 04/47 Crw | 68A | 10/67 | 44815 | 4815 | 11/44 Der | 13A | 02/68 |
| 44771 | 4771 | 05/47 Crw | 6A | 03/67 | 44816 | 4816 | 11/44 Der | 24C | 07/68 |
| 44772 | 4772 | 05/47 Crw | 8A | 10/67 | 44817 | 4817 | 11/44 Der | 68A | 08/67 |
| 44773 | 4773 | 05/47 Crw | 8A | 12/67 | 44818 | 4818 | 11/44 Der | 26A | 06/68 |
| 44774 | 4774 | 05/47 Crw | 8A | 08/67 | 44819 | 4819 | 11/44 Der | 10A | 11/67 |
| 44775 | 4775 | 06/47 Crw | 68A | 10/67 | 44820 | 4820 | 12/44 Der | 66B | 12/66 |
| 44776 | 4776 | 06/47 Crw | 10A | 10/67 | 44821 | 4821 | 12/44 Der | 5B | 06/67 |
| 44777 | 4777 | 06/47 Crw | 10C | 06/68 | 44822 | 4822 | 12/44 Der | 26A | 10/67 |
| 44778 | 4778 | 06/47 Crw | 11A | 11/67 | 44823 | 4823 | 12/44 Der | 10A | 11/65 |
| 44779 | 4779 | 07/47 Crw | 8B | 12/66 | 44824 | 4824 | 12/44 Der | 20D | 10/67 |
| 44780 | 4780 | 07/47 Crw | 26A | 06/68 | 44825 | 4825 | 12/44 Der | 68A | 10/67 |
| 44781 | 4781 | 08/47 Crw | 11A | 08/68 | 44826 | 4826 o | 07/44 Crw | 20A | 10/67 |
| 44782 | 4782 | 08/47 Crw | 9B | 12/66 | 44827 | 4827 o | 07/44 Crw | 8A | 07/65 |
| 44783 | 4783 | 03/47 Hor | 60A | 05/64 | 44828 | 4828 | 07/44 Crw | 20A | 09/67 |
| 44784 | 4784 | 04/47 Hor | 68B | 06/64 | 44829 | 4829 o | 08/44 Crw | 26C | 05/68 |
| 44785 | 4785 | 04/47 Hor | 67A | 06/64 | 44830 | 4830 o | 08/44 Crw | 13C | 08/67 |
| 44786 | 4786 | 04/47 Hor | 66B | 08/66 | 44831 | 4831 | 08/44 Crw | 10A | 11/67 |
| 44787 | 4787 | 05/47 Hor | 66B | 11/65 | 44832 | 4832 | 08/44 Crw | 5B | 09/67 |
| 44788 | 4788 | 05/47 Hor | 67C | 11/66 | 44833 | 4833 | 08/44 Crw | 5B | 09/67 |
| 44789 | 4789 | 05/47 Hor | 67B | 12/64 | 44834 | 4834 | 08/44 Crw | 8A | 12/67 |
| 44790 | 4790 | 06/47 Hor | 68A | 03/67 | 44835 | 4835 | 09/44 Crw | 13A | 07/67 |
| 44791 | 4791 | 06/47 Hor | 64D | 11/66 | 44836 | 4836 | 09/44 Crw | 9B | 05/68 |
| 44792 | 4792 | 07/47 Hor | 68A | 09/67 | 44837 | 4837 | 09/44 Crw | 8A | 09/67 |

## Appendix – Locomotives 44838-44927

| Number BR | LMSR | Built Date/Works | Last Shed/ Withdrawn | | Number BR | LMSR | Built Date Works | Last Shed Withdrawn | |
|---|---|---|---|---|---|---|---|---|---|
| 44838 | 4838 | 09/44 Crw | 8A | 03/68 | 44883 | 4883 | 06/45 Crw | 68A | 07/67 |
| 44839 | 4839 | 09/44 Crw | 13C | 12/66 | 44884 | 4884 | 06/45 Crw | 26A | 06/68 |
| 44840 | 4840 | 10/44 Crw | 6C | 11/67 | 44885 | 4885 | 07/45 Crw | 68B | 12/63 |
| 44841 | 4841 | 10/44 Crw | 84B | 10/66 | 44886 | 4886 | 07/45 Crw | 68A | 10/67 |
| 44842 | 4842 | 10/44 Crw | 9B | 01/68 | 44887 | 4887 | 08/45 Crw | 68A | 12/67 |
| 44843 | 4843 | 10/44 Crw | 5B | 09/67 | 44888 | 4888 | 08/45 Crw | 24C | 08/68 |
| 44844 | 4844 o | 10/44 Crw | 6C | 11/67 | 44889 | 4889 | 08/45 Crw | 11A | 01/68 |
| 44845 | 4845 | 10/44 Crw | 26A | 06/68 | 44890 | 4890 | 08/45 Crw | 26A | 06/68 |
| 44846 | 4846 | 11/44 Crw | 26A | 01/68 | 44891 | 4891 | 08/45 Crw | 26A | 06/68 |
| 44847 | 4847 | 11/44 Crw | 38A | 11/66 | 44892 | 4892 | 09/45 Crw | 11A | 04/67 |
| 44848 | 4848 | 11/44 Crw | 24B | 02/68 | 44893 | 4893 | 09/45 Crw | 26A | 11/67 |
| 44849 | 4849 | 11/44 Crw | 20A | 12/64 | 44894 | 4894 | 09/45 Crw | 11A | 08/68 |
| 44850 | 4850 | 11/44 Crw | 66B | 07/66 | 44895 | 4895 | 09/45 Crw | 13A | 12/67 |
| 44851 | 4851 | 11/44 Crw | 26A | 04/68 | 44896 | 4896 | 09/45 Crw | 20A | 09/67 |
| 44852 | 4852 | 11/44 Crw | 20A | 09/67 | 44897 | 4897 | 09/45 Crw | 11A | 08/68 |
| 44853 | 4853 | 11/44 Crw | 20A | 06/67 | 44898 | 4898 | 09/45 Crw | 68A | 10/67 |
| 44854 | 4854 | 12/44 Crw | 20D | 10/67 | 44899 | 4899 | 09/45 Crw | 24B | 07/68 |
| 44855 | 4855 | 12/44 Crw | 9B | 05/68 | 44900 | 4900 | 10/45 Crw | 68A | 06/67 |
| 44856 | 4856 | 12/44 Crw | 84B | 02/67 | 44901 | 4901 P | 10/45 Crw | 68A | 08/65 |
| 44857 | 4857 | 12/44 Crw | 20D | 10/67 | 44902 | 4902 | 10/45 Crw | 68A | 10/67 |
| 44858 | 4858 | 12/44 Crw | 68A | 12/67 | 44903 | 4903 | 10/45 Crw | 13C | 04/68 |
| 44859 | 4859 | 12/44 Crw | 6C | 11/67 | 44904 | 4904 | 10/45 Crw | 11A | 12/65 |
| 44860 | 4860 | 12/44 Crw | 5D | 01/67 | 44905 | 4905 | 10/45 Crw | 11A | 11/67 |
| 44861 | 4861 | 01/45 Crw | 26A | 11/67 | 44906 | 4906 | 10/45 Crw | 8A | 03/68 |
| 44862 | 4862 | 01/45 Crw | 68A | 07/67 | 44907 | 4907 | 11/45 Crw | 8A | 10/67 |
| 44863 | 4863 | 01/45 Crw | 8A | 05/67 | 44908 | 4908 | 11/45 Crw | 66B | 06/66 |
| 44864 | 4864 | 01/45 Crw | 8A | 05/68 | 44909 | 4909 | 11/45 Crw | 24B | 09/67 |
| 44865 | 4865 | 02/45 Crw | 5B | 09/67 | 44910 | 4910 | 11/45 Crw | 26A | 06/68 |
| 44866 | 4866 o | 02/45 Crw | 13A | 09/67 | 44911 | 4911 | 11/45 Crw | 68A | 10/67 |
| 44867 | 4867 | 02/45 Crw | 9B | 06/67 | 44912 | 4912 | 11/45 Crw | 20A | 09/67 |
| 44868 | 4868 | 02/45 Crw | 9B | 05/68 | 44913 | 4913 | 11/45 Crw | 6C | 07/67 |
| 44869 | 4869 | 03/45 Crw | 13C | 09/66 | 44914 | 4914 | 12/45 Crw | 13C | 08/67 |
| 44870 | 4870 | 03/45 Crw | 24B | 06/67 | 44915 | 4915 | 12/45 Crw | 24C | 12/67 |
| 44871 | 4871 P | 03/45 Crw | 11A | 08/68 | 44916 | 4916 | 12/45 Crw | 9B | 12/67 |
| 44872 | 4872 | 03/45 Crw | 24C | 09/67 | 44917 | 4917 | 12/45 Crw | 5B | 11/67 |
| 44873 | 4873 | 03/45 Crw | 10A | 11/67 | 44918 | 4918 | 12/45 Crw | 13A | 01/67 |
| 44874 | 4874 | 04/45 Crw | 11A | 08/68 | 44919 | 4919 | 12/45 Crw | 84B | 12/66 |
| 44875 | 4875 | 04/45 Crw | 6A | 05/67 | 44920 | 4920 | 12/45 Crw | 10A | 11/67 |
| 44876 | 4876 | 04/45 Crw | 6C | 11/67 | 44921 | 4921 | 01/46 Crw | 63A | 02/65 |
| 44877 | 4877 | 04/45 Crw | 11A | 08/68 | 44922 | 4922 | 01/46 Crw | 65B | 05/64 |
| 44878 | 4878 | 05/45 Crw | 24C | 07/68 | 44923 | 4923 | 01/46 Crw | 65B | 06/64 |
| 44879 | 4879 | 05/45 Crw | 62A | 04/67 | 44924 | 4924 | 02/46 Crw | 63A | 07/65 |
| 44880 | 4880 | 05/45 Crw | 66B | 11/66 | 44925 | 4925 | 02/46 Crw | 64A | 09/66 |
| 44881 | 4881 | 05/45 Crw | 66B | 07/66 | 44926 | 4926 | 02/46 Crw | 8A | 04/68 |
| 44882 | 4882 | 06/45 Crw | 68A | 07/67 | 44927 | 4927 | 02/46 Crw | 26C | 09/67 |

## Appendix - Locomotives 44928-45017

| Number BR | LMSR | Built Date/Works | Last Shed/ Withdrawn | | Number BR | LMSR | Built Date/Works | Last Shed/ Withdrawn | |
|---|---|---|---|---|---|---|---|---|---|
| 44928 | 4928 | 03/46 Crw | 12A | 06/67 | 44973 | 4973 | 05/46 Crw | 64D | 09/65 |
| 44929 | 4929 | 03/46 Crw | 9K | 06/68 | 44974 | 4974 | 05/46 Crw | 67C | 06/66 |
| 44930 | 4930 | 03/46 Crw | 8B | 05/67 | 44975 | 4975 | 05/46 Crw | 64C | 09/65 |
| 44931 | 4931 | 04/46 Crw | 63A | 10/65 | 44976 | 4976 | 05/46 Crw | 64C | 02/64 |
| 44932 | 4932 | 09/45 Hor | 24B | 08/68 P | 44977 | 4977 | 06/46 Crw | 67C | 11/66 |
| 44933 | 4933 | 10/45 Hor | 8A | 10/67 | 44978 | 4978 | 06/46 Crw | 63A | 07/65 |
| 44934 | 4934 | 10/45 Hor | 8B | 09/67 | 44979 | 4979 | 06/46 Crw | 63A | 07/65 |
| 44935 | 4935 | 10/45 Hor | 8B | 10/66 | 44980 | 4980 | 06/46 Crw | 63A | 07/65 |
| 44936 | 4936 | 11/45 Hor | 68A | 08/67 | 44981 | 4981 | 07/46 Crw | 84G | 01/67 |
| 44937 | 4937 | 11/45 Hor | 68A | 05/67 | 44982 | 4982 | 09/46 Crw | 68A | 05/67 |
| 44938 | 4938 | 11/45 Hor | 26A | 10/67 | 44983 | 4983 | 09/46 Hor | 20A | 10/67 |
| 44939 | 4939 | 11/45 Hor | 12A | 12/65 | 44984 | 4984 | 09/46 Hor | 38A | 11/66 |
| 44940 | 4940 | 11/45 Hor | 9B | 03/68 | 44985 | 4985 | 10/46 Hor | 10A | 10/67 |
| 44941 | 4941 | 12/45 Hor | 38A | 11/66 | 44986 | 4986 | 10/46 Hor | 68A | 05/67 |
| 44942 | 4942 | 12/45 Hor | 24C | 06/68 | 44987 | 4987 | 11/46 Hor | 11A | 10/66 |
| 44943 | 4943 | 12/45 Hor | 20A | 10/67 | 44988 | 4988 | 12/46 Hor | 9B | 12/67 |
| 44944 | 4944 | 01/46 Hor | 5B | 05/67 | 44989 | 4989 | 12/46 Hor | 68A | 02/67 |
| 44945 | 4945 | 01/46 Hor | 84B | 10/66 | 44990 | 4990 | 12/46 Hor | 20D | 10/67 |
| 44946 | 4946 | 01/46 Hor | 25A | 05/67 | 44991 | 4991 | 12/46 Hor | 66B | 05/67 |
| 44947 | 4947 | 02/46 Hor | 26C | 06/68 | 44992 | 4992 | 01/47 Hor | 67B | 12/66 |
| 44948 | 4948 | 02/46 Hor | 11A | 09/67 | 44993 | 4993 | 01/47 Hor | 68A | 12/67 |
| 44949 | 4949 | 02/46 Hors | 26A | 06/68 | 44994 | 4994 | 01/47 Hor | 64C | 07/64 |
| 44950 | 4950 | 03/46 Hor | 24C | 08/68 | 44995 | 4995 | 02/47 Hor | 67A | 11/66 |
| 44951 | 4951 | 03/46 Hor | 25A | 12/66 | 44996 | 4996 | 02/47 Hor | 68B | 04/64 |
| 44952 | 4952 | 03/46 Hor | 64D | 10/66 | 44997 | 4997 | 03/47 Hor | 63A | 05/67 |
| 44953 | 4953 | 03/46 Hor | 64D | 12/66 | 44998 | 4998 | 03/47 Hor | 63A | 04/67 |
| 44954 | 4954 | 04/46 Hor | 64D | 09/66 | 44999 | 4999 | 03/47 Hor | 68C | 09/66 |
| 44955 | 4955 | 04/46 Hor | 67B | 07/65 | 45000 | 5000 P | 03/35 Crw | 24C | 10/67 |
| 44956 | 4956 | 04/46 Hor | 64D | 06/66 | 45001 | 5001 | 04/35 Crw | 11A | 03/68 |
| 44957 | 4957 | 05/46 Hor | 68B | 05/64 | 45002 | 5002 | 04/35 Crw | 5B | 07/65 |
| 44958 | 4958 | 05/46 Hor | 24C | 03/67 | 45003 | 5003 | 04/35 Crw | 5D | 06/67 |
| 44959 | 4959 | 05/46 Hor | 63A | 07/65 | 45004 | 5004 | 04/35 Crw | 7A | 09/66 |
| 44960 | 4960 | 05/46 Hor | 63A | 01/66 | 45005 | 5005 | 04/35 Crw | 8A | 01/68 |
| 44961 | 4961 | 06/46 Hor | 63A | 06/64 | 45006 | 5006 | 04/35 Crw | 5B | 09/67 |
| 44962 | 4962 | 06/46 Hor | 26A | 12/67 | 45007 | 5007 | 04/35 Crw | 67B | 07/64 |
| 44963 | 4963 | 06/46 Crw | 11A | 07/68 | 45008 | 5008 | 04/35 Crw | 66B | 05/64 |
| 44964 | 4964 | 07/46 Crw | 8A | 10/67 | 45009 | 5009 | 04/35 Crw | 66B | 11/65 |
| 44965 | 4965 | 08/46 Crw | 26C | 04/68 | 45010 | 5010 | 04/35 Crw | 67B | 08/63 |
| 44966 | 4966 | 08/46 Crw | 84G | 09/66 | 45011 | 5011 | 04/35 Crw | 64D | 12/65 |
| 44967 | 4967 | 04/46 Crw | 68B | 05/64 | 45012 | 5012 | 04/35 Crw | 11D | 10/66 |
| 44968 | 4968 | 04/46 Crw | 66B | 05/64 | 45013 | 5013 | 04/35 Crw | 9B | 05/68 |
| 44969 | 4969 | 04/46 Crw | 66B | 12/63 | 45014 | 5014 | 04/35 Crw | 11A | 06/67 |
| 44970 | 4970 | 04/46 Crw | 65A | 09/65 | 45015 | 5015 | 04/35 Crw | 8A | 09/67 |
| 44971 | 4971 | 04/46 Crw | 24C | 08/68 | 45016 | 5016 | 05/35 Crw | 67C | 07/66 |
| 44972 | 4972 | 04/46 Crw | 67B | 11/66 | 45017 | 5017 | 05/35 Crw | 11A | 08/68 |

## Appendix - Locomotives 45018-45107

| Number BR | LMSR | Built Date/Works | Last Shed/ Withdrawn | | Number BR | LMSR | Built Date/Works | Last Shed/ Withdrawn | |
|---|---|---|---|---|---|---|---|---|---|
| 45018 | 5018 | 05/35 Crw | 68A | 12/66 | 45063 | 5063 | 12/34 VF | 20A | 10/66 |
| 45019 | 5019 | 05/35 Crw | 10A | 05/67 | 45064 | 5064 | 12/34 VF | 6A | 03/67 |
| 45020 | 5020 | 08/34 VF | 5D | 12/65 | 45065 | 5065 | 12/34 VF | 13C | 05/68 |
| 45021 | 5021 | 08/34 VF | 5B | 19/67 | 45066 | 5066 | 01/35 VF | 66A | 02/64 |
| 45022 | 5022 | 08/34 VF | 64C | 09/63 | 45067 | 5067 | 01/35 VF | 13C | 10/67 |
| 45023 | 5023 | 08/34 VF | 64C | 09/63 | 45068 | 5068 | 01/35 VF | 8B | 12/65 |
| 45024 | 5024 | 08/34 VF | 10A | 05/67 | 45069 | 5069 | 01/35 VF | 8A | 06/67 |
| 45025 | 5025 P | 08/34 VF | 11A | 08/68 | 45070 | 5070 | 05/35 Crw | 8B | 05/67 |
| 45026 | 5026 | 09/34 VF | 26A | 10/65 | 45071 | 5071 | 05/35 Crw | 8C | 07/67 |
| 45027 | 5027 | 09/34 VF | 9B | 05/68 | 45072 | 5072 | 06/35 Crw | 11A | 09/67 |
| 45028 | 5028 | 09/34 VF | 68A | 03/67 | 45073 | 5073 | 06/35 Crw | 24C | 08/68 |
| 45029 | 5029 | 09/34 VF | 66B | 10/66 | 45074 | 5074 | 06/35 Crw | 5D | 09/65 |
| 45030 | 5030 | 09/34 VF | 64C | 12/62 | 45075 | 5075 | 02/35 VF | 20D | 09/67 |
| 45031 | 5031 | 09/34 VF | 8C | 06/67 | 45076 | 5076 | 03/35 VF | 26A | 06/68 |
| 45032 | 5032 | 09/34 VF | 8A | 02/64 | 45077 | 5077 | 03/35 VF | 26A | 08/65 |
| 45033 | 5033 | 09/34 VF | 5B | 12/66 | 45078 | 5078 | 03/35 VF | 5D | 10/65 |
| 45034 | 5034 | 09/34 VF | 8C | 02/68 | 45079 | 5079 | 03/35 VF | 20A | 03/67 |
| 45035 | 5035 | 09/34 VF | 28B | 11/64 | 45080 | 5080 | 03/35 VF | 20A | 10/67 |
| 45036 | 5036 | 09/34 VF | 64C | 12/62 | 45081 | 5081 | 03/35 VF | 12A | 10/65 |
| 45037 | 5037 | 09/34 VF | 5D | 11/65 | 45082 | 5082 | 03/35 VF | 68A | 07/66 |
| 45038 | 5038 | 09/34 VF | 9B | 02/68 | 45083 | 5083 | 03/35 VF | 26A | 12/67 |
| 45039 | 5039 | 10/34 VF | 8A | 08/67 | 45084 | 5084 | 03/35 VF | 64D | 11/66 |
| 45040 | 5040 | 10/34 VF | 5B | 07/67 | 45085 | 5085 | 03/35 VF | 66B | 12/62 |
| 45041 | 5041 | 10/34 VF | 24C | 12/67 | 45086 | 5086 | 03/35 VF | 64C | 12/62 |
| 45042 | 5042 | 10/34 VF | 5B | 09/67 | 45087 | 5087 | 03/35 VF | 64D | 07/63 |
| 45043 | 5043 | 10/34 VF | 8C | 11/67 | 45088 | 5088 | 04/35 VF | 17A | 09/64 |
| 45044 | 5044 | 10/34 VF | 6A | 10/66 | 45089 | 5089 | 04/35 VF | 5B | 08/67 |
| 45045 | 5045 | 10/34 VF | 13C | 10/66 | 45090 | 5090 | 04/35 VF | 64D | 12/65 |
| 45046 | 5046 | 10/34 VF | 26C | 06/68 | 45091 | 5091 | 04/35 VF | 10A | 09/66 |
| 45047 | 5047 | 10/34 VF | 64A | 07/66 | 45092 | 5092 | 04/35 VF | 11A | 12/67 |
| 45048 | 5048 | 10/34 VF | 10A | 11/67 | 45093 | 5093 | 04/35 VF | 5C | 10/65 |
| 45049 | 5049 | 11/34 VF | 63B | 08/63 | 45094 | 5094 | 04/35 VF | 8A | 02/67 |
| 45050 | 5050 | 11/34 VF | 5D | 08/67 | 45095 | 5095 | 04/35 VF | 11A | 08/68 |
| 45051 | 5051 | 11/34 VF | 84G | 11/66 | 45096 | 5096 | 04/35 VF | 24B | 08/68 |
| 45052 | 5052 | 11/34 VF | 5B | 09/67 | 45097 | 5097 | 04/35 VF | 68A | 06/66 |
| 45053 | 5053 | 11/34 VF | 64A | 11/66 | 45098 | 5098 | 04/35 VF | 66A | 12/62 |
| 45054 | 5054 | 11/34 VF | 11A | 02/68 | 45099 | 5099 | 04/35 VF | 66B | 09/63 |
| 45055 | 5055 | 11/34 VF | 24C | 08/68 | 45100 | 5100 | 05/35 VF | 68A | 10/63 |
| 45056 | 5056 | 11/34 VF | 8C | 08/67 | 45101 | 5101 | 05/35 VF | 26A | 03/68 |
| 45057 | 5057 | 12/34 VF | 8C | 08/67 | 45102 | 5102 | 05/35 VF | 5A | 01/65 |
| 45058 | 5058 | 12/34 VF | 84G | 10/66 | 45103 | 5103 | 05/35 VF | 8A | 09/64 |
| 45059 | 5059 | 12/34 VF | 8C | 07/67 | 45104 | 5104 | 05/35 VF | 26C | 06/68 |
| 45060 | 5060 | 12/34 VF | 5D | 03/67 | 45105 | 5105 | 05/35 VF | 68A | 10/66 |
| 45061 | 5061 | 12/34 VF | 68A | 11/67 | 45106 | 5106 | 05/35 VF | 68A | 01/67 |
| 45062 | 5062 | 12/34 VF | 13A | 04/67 | 45107 | 5107 | 05/35 VF | 24C | 09/67 |

## Appendix - Locomotives 45108-45197

| Number BR | LMSR | Built Date/Works | Last Shed/ Withdrawn | | Number BR | LMSR | Built Date/Works | Last Shed/ Withdrawn | |
|---|---|---|---|---|---|---|---|---|---|
| 45108 | 5108 | 05/35 VF | 10A | 12/65 | 45153 | 5153 | 06/35 AW | 68B | 05/64 |
| 45109 | 5109 | 05/35 VF | 8B | 04/67 | 45154 | 5154 | 06/35 AW | 8C | 11/66 |
| 45110 | 5110 P | 06/35 VF | 24C | 08/68 | 45155 | 5155 | 07/35 AW | 64C | 11/64 |
| 45111 | 5111 | 06/35 VF | 24B | 10/67 | 45156 | 5156 | 07/35 AW | 24B | 08/68 |
| 45112 | 5112 | 06/35 VF | 68A | 10/66 | 45157 | 5157 | 07/35 AW | 65B | 12/62 |
| 45113 | 5113 | 06/35 VF | 2B | 07/65 | 45158 | 5158 | 07/35 AW | 68B | 07/64 |
| 45114 | 5114 | 06/35 VF | 13C | 01/68 | 45159 | 5159 | 07/35 AW | 65B | 04/63 |
| 45115 | 5115 | 06/35 VF | 67B | 11/66 | 45160 | 5160 | 07/35 AW | 67C | 09/66 |
| 45116 | 5116 | 06/35 VF | 10A | 07/67 | 45161 | 5161 | 07/35 AW | 64D | 11/66 |
| 45117 | 5117 | 06/35 VF | 67B | 10/65 | 45162 | 5162 | 08/35 AW | 64A | 11/66 |
| 45118 | 5118 | 06/35 VF | 68A | 10/66 | 45163 | 5163 P | 08/35 AW | 68A | 05/65 |
| 45119 | 5119 | 06/35 VF | 65B | 12/62 | 45164 | 5164 | 08/35 AW | 67C | 08/66 |
| 45120 | 5120 | 06/35 VF | 68A | 06/67 | 45165 | 5165 | 08/35 AW | 66B | 12/62 |
| 45121 | 5121 | 06/35 VF | 66B | 05/64 | 45166 | 5166 | 08/35 AW | 64D | 09/63 |
| 45122 | 5122 | 06/35 VF | 68A | 04/64 | 45167 | 5167 | 08/35 AW | 66B | 05/67 |
| 45123 | 5123 | 07/35 VF | 67B | 09/63 | 45168 | 5168 | 08/35 AW | 64A | 09/66 |
| 45124 | 5124 | 07/35 VF | 66A | 05/67 | 45169 | 5169 | 08/35 AW | 68B | 05/63 |
| 45125 | 5125 | 05/35 AW | 65F | 05/63 | 45170 | 5170 | 08/35 AW | 64C | 03/64 |
| 45126 | 5126 | 05/35 AW | 68A | 05/67 | 45171 | 5171 | 08/35 AW | 64D | 10/65 |
| 45127 | 5127 | 05/35 AW | 62B | 11/66 | 45172 | 5172 | 08/35 AW | 64D | 05/64 |
| 45128 | 5128 | 05/35 AW | 10A | 09/66 | 45173 | 5173 | 08/35 AW | 64D | 07/64 |
| 45129 | 5129 | 05/35 AW | 8B | 09/66 | 45174 | 5174 | 08/35 AW | 64D | 03/63 |
| 45130 | 5130 | 05/35 AW | 6C | 11/67 | 45175 | 5175 | 08/35 AW | 64D | 07/63 |
| 45131 | 5131 | 05/35 AW | 8C | 04/68 | 45176 | 5176 | 08/35 AW | 66B | 08/66 |
| 45132 | 5132 | 05/35 AW | 84G | 03/67 | 45177 | 5177 | 09/35 AW | 67C | 07/66 |
| 45133 | 5133 | 05/35 AW | 8A | 02/68 | 45178 | 5178 | 09/35 AW | 66B | 01/65 |
| 45134 | 5134 | 05/35 AW | 11A | 08/68 | 45179 | 5179 | 09/35 AW | 66B | 06/63 |
| 45135 | 5135 | 05/35 AW | 68A | 10/67 | 45180 | 5180 | 09/35 AW | 5B | 09/65 |
| 45136 | 5136 | 05/35 AW | 63A | 10/64 | 45181 | 5181 | 09/35 AW | 8C | 01/66 |
| 45137 | 5137 | 06/35 AW | 8C | 12/66 | 45182 | 5182 | 09/35 AW | 11B | 03/66 |
| 45138 | 5138 | 06/35 AW | 68A | 09/66 | 45183 | 5183 | 09/35 AW | 64C | 10/64 |
| 45139 | 5139 | 06/35 AW | 9B | 08/67 | 45184 | 5184 | 09/35 AW | 6A | 09/65 |
| 45140 | 5140 | 06/35 AW | 10A | 09/66 | 45185 | 5185 | 09/35 AW | 68A | 06/66 |
| 45141 | 5141 | 06/35 AW | 24C | 03/67 | 45186 | 5186 | 09/35 AW | 5B | 09/67 |
| 45142 | 5142 | 06/35 AW | 5B | 04/65 | 45187 | 5187 | 09/35 AW | 10C | 06/68 |
| 45143 | 5143 | 06/35 AW | 84G | 12/65 | 45188 | 5188 | 09/35 AW | 8C | 07/67 |
| 45144 | 5144 | 06/35 AW | 17A | 06/64 | 45189 | 5189 | 09/35 AW | 5A | 07/63 |
| 45145 | 5145 | 06/35 AW | 5B | 11/67 | 45190 | 5190 | 10/35 AW | 13C | 05/68 |
| 45146 | 5146 | 06/35 AW | 5D | 06/65 | 45191 | 5191 | 10/35 AW | 5D | 07/67 |
| 45147 | 5147 | 06/35 AW | 27B | 05/67 | 45192 | 5192 | 10/35 AW | 65F | 08/65 |
| 45148 | 5148 | 06/35 AW | 68A | 12/65 | 45193 | 5193 | 10/35 AW | 11A | 08/67 |
| 45149 | 5149 | 06/35 AW | 24C | 06/68 | 45194 | 5194 | 10/35 AW | 67C | 04/65 |
| 45150 | 5150 | 06/35 AW | 13A | 03/68 | 45195 | 5195 | 10/35 AW | 68A | 07/66 |
| 45151 | 5151 | 06/35 AW | 66B | 12/62 | 45196 | 5196 | 10/35 AW | 24B | 12/67 |
| 45152 | 5152 | 06/35 AW | 66B | 12/62 | 45197 | 5197 | 10/35 AW | 24C | 01/67 |

## Appendix – Locomotives 45198-45287

| Number BR | LMSR | Built Date/Works | Last Shed/ Withdrawn | | Number BR | LMSR | Built Date/Works | Last Shed/ Withdrawn | |
|---|---|---|---|---|---|---|---|---|---|
| 45198 | 5198 | 10/35 AW | 10A | 09/67 | 45243 | 5243 | 09/36 AW | 5B | 09/67 |
| 45199 | 5199 | 10/35 AW | 17B | 09/63 | 45244 | 5244 | 09/36 AW | 8A | 08/63 |
| 45200 | 5200 | 10/35 AW | 11A | 07/68 | 45245 | 5245 | 09/36 AW | 64D | 08/65 |
| 45201 | 5201 | 10/35 AW | 8C | 05/68 | 45246 | 5246 | 09/36 AW | 26A | 12/67 |
| 45202 | 5202 | 10/35 AW | 26A | 06/68 | 45247 | 5247 | 09/36 AW | 6A | 04/67 |
| 45203 | 5203 | 11/35 AW | 26A | 06/68 | 45248 | 5248 | 09/36 AW | 5B | 02/66 |
| 45204 | 5204 | 11/35 AW | 20A | 01/67 | 45249 | 5249 | 09/36 AW | 8A | 12/66 |
| 45205 | 5205 | 11/35 AW | 26A | 10/66 | 45250 | 5250 | 09/36 AW | 6A | 03/67 |
| 45206 | 5206 | 11/35 AW | 11A | 08/68 | 45251 | 5251 | 09/36 AW | 67D | 12/63 |
| 45207 | 5207 | 11/35 AW | 20C | 09/66 | 45252 | 5252 | 09/36 AW | 26C | 03/66 |
| 45208 | 5208 | 11/35 AW | 24F | 10/67 | 45253 | 5253 | 09/36 AW | 13C | 04/68 |
| 45209 | 5209 | 11/35 AW | 11A | 06/68 | 45254 | 5254 | 09/36 AW | 26A | 05/68 |
| 45210 | 5210 | 11/35 AW | 68A | 04/66 | 45255 | 5255 | 10/36 AW | 26A | 06/68 |
| 45211 | 5211 | 11/35 AW | 20A | 05/67 | 45256 | 5256 | 10/36 AW | 8B | 06/67 |
| 45212 | 5212 P | 11/35 AW | 24C | 08/68 | 45257 | 5257 | 10/36 AW | 5D | 10/65 |
| 45213 | 5213 | 11/35 AW | 66B | 12/66 | 45258 | 5258 | 10/36 AW | 13A | 03/68 |
| 45214 | 5214 | 11/35 AW | 67A | 12/66 | 45259 | 5259 | 10/36 AW | 68A | 12/67 |
| 45215 | 5215 | 11/35 AW | 24B | 10/67 | 45260 | 5260 | 10/36 AW | 24C | 08/68 |
| 45216 | 5216 | 11/35 AW | 24B | 02/66 | 45261 | 5261 | 10/36 AW | 9B | 10/67 |
| 45217 | 5217 | 11/35 AW | 68A | 11/66 | 45262 | 5262 | 10/36 AW | 24B | 08/68 |
| 45218 | 5218 | 11/35 AW | 68A | 04/66 | 45263 | 5263 | 10/36 AW | 13C | 10/67 |
| 45219 | 5219 | 11/35 AW | 20A | 10/67 | 45264 | 5264 | 10/36 AW | 5B | 09/67 |
| 45220 | 5220 | 11/35 AW | 13A | 09/66 | 45265 | 5265 | 10/36 AW | 21A | 05/62 |
| 45221 | 5221 | 11/35 AW | 9B | 12/67 | 45266 | 5266 | 10/36 AW | 67B | 12/62 |
| 45222 | 5222 | 12/35 AW | 26A | 02/67 | 45267 | 5267 | 10/36 AW | 10A | 10/67 |
| 45223 | 5223 | 12/35 AW | 8C | 12/66 | 45268 | 5268 | 10/36 AW | 11A | 08/68 |
| 45224 | 5224 | 12/35 AW | 38A | 11/66 | 45269 | 5269 | 11/36 AW | 24C | 08/68 |
| 45225 | 5225 | 08/36 AW | 9B | 10/67 | 45270 | 5270 | 11/36 AW | 5B | 09/67 |
| 45226 | 5226 | 08/36 AW | 24C | 09/67 | 45271 | 5271 | 11/36 AW | 26A | 09/67 |
| 45227 | 5227 | 08/36 AW | 24C | 01/68 | 45272 | 5272 | 11/36 AW | 84B | 10/65 |
| 45228 | 5228 | 08/36 AW | 68A | 03/67 | 45273 | 5273 | 11/36 AW | 20A | 10/67 |
| 45229 | 5229 | 08/36 AW | 27B | 09/65 | 45274 | 5274 | 11/36 AW | 68A | 05/67 |
| 45230 | 5230 | 08/36 AW | 11A | 08/65 | 45275 | 5275 | 11/36 AW | 24B | 10/67 |
| 45231 | 5231 P | 08/36 AW | 11A | 08/68 | 45276 | 5276 | 11/36 AW | 5D | 01/67 |
| 45232 | 5232 | 08/36 AW | 6C | 11/67 | 45277 | 5277 | 11/36 AW | 6A | 02/67 |
| 45233 | 5233 | 08/36 AW | 13A | 05/66 | 45278 | 5278 | 11/36 AW | 10A | 06/67 |
| 45234 | 5234 | 08/36 AW | 26A | 09/67 | 45279 | 5279 | 11/36 AW | 13C | 03/68 |
| 45235 | 5235 | 08/36 AW | 68A | 01/66 | 45280 | 5280 | 11/36 AW | 6C | 11/67 |
| 45236 | 5236 | 08/36 AW | 68A | 12/67 | 45281 | 5281 | 11/36 AW | 10A | 11/67 |
| 45237 | 5237 | 08/36 AW | 6B | 09/65 | 45282 | 5282 | 11/36 AW | 8A | 05/68 |
| 45238 | 5238 | 08/36 AW | 8B | 12/66 | 45283 | 5283 | 11/36 AW | 84B | 01/67 |
| 45239 | 5239 | 08/36 AW | 13A | 09/67 | 45284 | 5284 | 12/36 AW | 8A | 05/68 |
| 45240 | 5240 | 08/36 AW | 5D | 01/67 | 45285 | 5285 | 12/36 AW | 68A | 12/67 |
| 45241 | 5241 | 09/36 AW | 5B | 09/67 | 45286 | 5286 | 12/36 AW | 11A | 03/65 |
| 45242 | 5242 | 09/36 AW | 8A | 06/67 | 45287 | 5287 | 12/36 AW | 24B | 08/68 |

## Appendix - Locomotives 45288-45377

| Number BR | LMSR | Built/ Date/Works | Last Shed/ Withdrawn | | Number BR | LMSR | Built Date/Works | Last Shed/ Withdrawn | |
|---|---|---|---|---|---|---|---|---|---|
| 45288 | 5288 | 12/36 AW | 6B | 11/67 | 45333 | 5333 | 03/37 AW | 13A | 06/66 |
| 45289 | 5289 | 12/36 AW | 38A | 11/66 | 45334 | 5334 | 03/37 AW | 38B | 07/65 |
| 45290 | 5290 | 12/36 AW | 26C | 06/68 | 45335 | 5335 | 03/37 AW | 38B | 07/65 |
| 45291 | 5291 | 12/36 AW | 26A | 10/65 | 45336 | 5336 | 03/37 AW | 26A | 01/67 |
| 45292 | 5292 | 12/36 AW | 6C | 11/67 | 45337 | 5337 P | 04/37 AW | 68A | 02/65 |
| 45293 | 5293 P | 12/36 AW | 68A | 08/65 | 45338 | 5338 | 04/37 AW | 8C | 10/66 |
| 45294 | 5294 | 12/36 AW | 26C | 03/68 | 45339 | 5339 | 04/37 AW | 24C | 06/67 |
| 45295 | 5295 | 12/36 AW | 68A | 12/67 | 45340 | 5340 | 04/37 AW | 68A | 04/67 |
| 45296 | 5296 | 12/36 AW | 8A | 02/68 | 45341 | 5341 | 04/37 AW | 26A | 01/67 |
| 45297 | 5297 | 12/36 AW | 5B | 09/67 | 45342 | 5342 | 04/37 AW | 11A | 08/68 |
| 45298 | 5298 | 12/36 AW | 5B | 09/67 | 45343 | 5343 | 04/37 AW | 24B | 06/67 |
| 45299 | 5299 | 01/37 AW | 6C | 11/67 | 45344 | 5344 | 04/37 AW | 84J | 08/66 |
| 45300 | 5300 | 01/37 AW | 7C | 12/65 | 45345 | 5345 | 04/37 AW | 24C | 06/68 |
| 45301 | 5301 | 01/37 AW | 38B | 07/65 | 45346 | 5346 | 04/37 AW | 9B | 06/67 |
| 45302 | 5302 | 01/37 AW | 5D | 07/67 | 45347 | 5347 | 04/37 AW | 24C | 11/67 |
| 45303 | 5303 | 01/37 AW | 8B | 06/67 | 45348 | 5348 | 04/37 AW | 84G | 08/66 |
| 45304 | 5304 | 01/37 AW | 26C | 08/67 | 45349 | 5349 | 05/37 AW | 5B | 11/67 |
| 45305 | 5305 P | 01/37 AW | 24C | 08/68 | 45350 | 5350 | 05/37 AW | 24B | 08/68 |
| 45306 | 5306 | 01/37 AW | 11A | 01/65 | 45351 | 5351 | 05/37 AW | 24C | 08/65 |
| 45307 | 5307 | 01/37 AW | 8A | 10/67 | 45352 | 5352 | 05/37 AW | 13A | 04/67 |
| 45308 | 5308 | 01/37 AW | 5D | 08/67 | 45353 | 5353 | 05/37 AW | 24C | 07/68 |
| 45309 | 5309 | 01/37 AW | 64D | 09/66 | 45354 | 5354 | 05/37 AW | 23C | 10/65 |
| 45310 | 5310 | 01/37 AW | 11A | 08/68 | 45355 | 5355 | 05/37 AW | 64B | 01/63 |
| 45311 | 5311 | 02/37 AW | 84G | 10/66 | 45356 | 5356 | 05/37 AW | 66B | 05/64 |
| 45312 | 5312 | 02/37 AW | 26C | 06/68 | 45357 | 5357 | 05/37 AW | 67A | 12/66 |
| 45313 | 5313 | 02/37 AW | 10A | 02/65 | 45358 | 5358 | 05/37 AW | 64C | 12/63 |
| 45314 | 5314 | 02/37 AW | 10A | 10/65 | 45359 | 5359 | 05/37 AW | 66B | 05/67 |
| 45315 | 5315 | 02/37 AW | 5B | 09/63 | 45360 | 5360 | 05/37 AW | 64C | 09/65 |
| 45316 | 5316 | 02/37 AW | 13A | 03/68 | 45361 | 5361 | 05/37 AW | 63B | 02/64 |
| 45317 | 5317 | 02/37 AW | 68A | 11/63 | 45362 | 5362 | 05/37 AW | 63B | 10/65 |
| 45318 | 5318 | 02/37 AW | 24C | 08/68 | 45363 | 5363 | 06/37 AW | 68A | 10/67 |
| 45319 | 5319 | 02/37 AW | 66B | 05/67 | 45364 | 5364 | 06/37 AW | 68A | 08/66 |
| 45320 | 5320 | 02/37 AW | 63B | 10/63 | 45365 | 5365 | 06/37 AW | 64D | 12/66 |
| 45321 | 5321 | 02/37 AW | 10A | 10/67 | 45366 | 5366 | 06/37 AW | 67A | 04/64 |
| 45322 | 5322 | 02/37 AW | 5D | 09/66 | 45367 | 5367 | 06/37 AW | 64C | 11/63 |
| 45323 | 5323 | 02/37 AW | 8B | 09/67 | 45368 | 5368 | 06/37 AW | 10A | 11/67 |
| 45324 | 5324 | 02/37 AW | 13C | 08/67 | 45369 | 5369 | 06/37 AW | 6A | 03/67 |
| 45325 | 5325 | 03/37 AW | 6A | 08/66 | 45370 | 5370 | 06/37 AW | 8C | 08/66 |
| 45326 | 5326 | 03/37 AW | 11A | 03/67 | 45371 | 5371 | 06/37 AW | 12D | 04/67 |
| 45327 | 5327 | 03/37 AW | 7A | 01/65 | 45372 | 5372 | 06/37 AW | 10A | 11/66 |
| 45328 | 5328 | 03/37 AW | 11A | 09/67 | 45373 | 5373 | 06/37 AW | 24C | 09/67 |
| 45329 | 5329 | 03/37 AW | 8C | 11/66 | 45374 | 5374 | 06/37 AW | 11A | 10/67 |
| 45330 | 5330 | 03/37 AW | 11A | 08/68 | 45375 | 5375 | 06/37 AW | 8A | 01/68 |
| 45331 | 5331 | 03/37 AW | 10A | 11/67 | 45376 | 5376 | 06/37 AW | 8A | 04/69 |
| 45332 | 5332 | 03/37 AW | 8C | 11/66 | 45377 | 5377 | 06/37 AW | 26C | 12/67 |

## Appendix - Locomotives 45378-45467

| Number BR | LMSR | Built Date/Works | Last Shed/ Withdrawn | | Number BR | LMSR | Built Date/Works | Last Shed/ Withdrawn | |
|---|---|---|---|---|---|---|---|---|---|
| 45378 | 5378 | 07/37 AW | 26C | 03/65 | 45423 | 5423 | 10/37 AW | 66B | 05/67 |
| 45379 | 5379 P | 07/37 AW | 1A | 07/65 | 45424 | 5424 | 10/37 AW | 11A | 04/68 |
| 45380 | 5380 | 07/37 AW | 13A | 03/65 | 45425 | 5425 | 10/37 AW | 10A | 10/67 |
| 45381 | 5381 | 07/37 AW | 26C | 05/68 | 45426 | 5426 | 10/37 AW | 8A | 03/68 |
| 45382 | 5382 | 07/37 AW | 24B | 06/68 | 45427 | 5427 | 10/37 AW | 6A | 08/66 |
| 45383 | 5383 | 07/37 AW | 68A | 02/67 | 45428 | 5428 P | 10/37 AW | 20A | 10/67 |
| 45384 | 5384 | 07/37 AW | 68C | 06/64 | 45429 | 5429 | 11/37 AW | 6A | 08/65 |
| 45385 | 5385 | 07/37 AW | 10A | 10/66 | 45430 | 5430 | 11/37 AW | 84G | 09/66 |
| 45386 | 5386 | 07/37 AW | 24C | 08/68 | 45431 | 5431 | 11/37 AW | 5B | 12/67 |
| 45387 | 5387 | 07/37 AW | 5D | 03/65 | 45432 | 5432 | 11/37 AW | 67C | 10/66 |
| 45388 | 5388 | 07/37 AW | 24C | 08/68 | 45433 | 5433 | 11/37 AW | 66B | 03/66 |
| 45389 | 5389 | 07/37 AW | 63B | 10/65 | 45434 | 5434 | 11/37 AW | 5B | 08/66 |
| 45390 | 5390 | 07/37 AW | 11A | 08/68 | 45435 | 5435 | 11/37 AW | 11A | 06/68 |
| 45391 | 5391 | 08/37 AW | 24C | 02/68 | 45436 | 5436 | 11/37 AW | 24C | 04/68 |
| 45392 | 5392 | 08/37 AW | 13C | 05/68 | 45437 | 5437 | 11/37 AW | 68A | 10/67 |
| 45393 | 5393 | 08/37AW | 5B | 09/66 | 45438 | 5438 | 11/37 AW | 6A | 08/66 |
| 45394 | 5394 | 08/37 AW | 11A | 07/68 | 45439 | 5439 | 11/37 AW | 3D | 11/65 |
| 45395 | 5395 | 08/37 AW | 8A | 03/68 | 45440 | 5440 | 11/37 AW | 8A | 09/67 |
| 45396 | 5396 | 08/37 AW | 63B | 02/66 | 45441 | 5441 | 12/37 AW | 8C | 02/67 |
| 45397 | 5397 | 08/37 AW | 24B | 08/68 | 45442 | 5442 | 12/37 AW | 68A | 08/66 |
| 45398 | 5398 | 08/37 AW | 4B | 09/65 | 45443 | 5443 | 12/37 AW | 65F | 08/65 |
| 45399 | 5399 | 08/37 AW | 11A | 12/66 | 45444 | 5444 | 12/37 AW | 24C | 08/68 |
| 45400 | 5400 | 08/37 AW | 63B | 05/64 | 45445 | 5445 | 12/37 AW | 11A | 06/68 |
| 45401 | 5401 | 08/37 AW | 8A | 11/61 | 45446 | 5446 | 12/37 AW | 5B | 02/67 |
| 45402 | 5402 | 08/37 AW | 24C | 04/67 | 45447 | 5447 | 12/37 AW | 24B | 08/68 |
| 45403 | 5403 | 08/37 AW | 6A | 09/66 | 45448 | 5448 | 12/37 AW | 13C | 08/67 |
| 45404 | 5404 | 08/37 AW | 2B | 05/67 | 45449 | 5449 | 12/37 AW | 10A | 11/67 |
| 45405 | 5405 | 09/37 AW | 5D | 08/67 | 45450 | 5450 | 12/37 AW | 24C | 11/67 |
| 45406 | 5406 | 09/37 AW | 8C | 07/67 | 45451 | 5451 | 12/37 AW | 12A | 11/66 |
| 45407 | 5407 P | 09/37 AW | 24C | 08/68 | 45452 | 5452 | 09/38 Crw | 64D | 06/63 |
| 45408 | 5408 | 09/37 AW | 10A | 11/66 | 45453 | 5453 | 09/38 Crw | 68B | 12/62 |
| 45409 | 5409 | 09/37 AW | 9B | 08/67 | 45454 | 5454 | 09/38 Crw | 13A | 08/67 |
| 45410 | 5410 | 09/37 AW | 21A | 09/66 | 45455 | 5455 | 09/38 Crw | 68A | 08/67 |
| 45411 | 5411 | 09/37 AW | 26A | 06/68 | 45456 | 5456 | 10/38 Crw | 68B | 12/64 |
| 45412 | 5412 | 09/37 AW | 8C | 08/67 | 45457 | 5457 | 10/38 Crw | 67D | 09/63 |
| 45413 | 5413 | 09/37 AW | 10C | 09/64 | 45458 | 5458 | 10/38 Crw | 66A | 12/62 |
| 45414 | 5414 | 10/37 AW | 8A | 02/65 | 45459 | 5459 | 10/38 Crw | 67B | 05/64 |
| 45415 | 5415 | 10/37 AW | 26C | 10/67 | 45460 | 5460 | 10/38 Crw | 67C | 06/65 |
| 45416 | 5416 | 10/37 AW | 38B | 07/65 | 45461 | 5461 | 10/38 Crw | 63A | 08/66 |
| 45417 | 5417 | 10/37 AW | 8C | 07/67 | 45462 | 5462 | 11/38 Crw | 66B | 06/64 |
| 45418 | 5418 | 10/37 AW | 84C | 02/66 | 45463 | 5463 | 11/38 Crw | 68C | 11/66 |
| 45419 | 5419 | 10/37 AW | 6A | 09/66 | 45464 | 5464 | 11/38 Crw | 38A | 10/66 |
| 45420 | 5420 | 10/37 AW | 26A | 06/68 | 45465 | 5465 | 11/38 Crw | 63A | 02/64 |
| 45421 | 5421 | 10/37 AW | 24C | 02/68 | 45466 | 5466 | 11/38 Crw | 8C | 02/67 |
| 45422 | 5422 | 10/37 AW | 5D | 09/66 | 45467 | 5467 | 11/38 Crw | 66B | 12/66 |

## Appendix – Locomotives 45468-45499

| Number BR | LMSR | Built Date/Works | Last Shed/ Withdrawn | | Number BR | LMSR | Built Date/Works | Last Shed/ Withdrawn | |
|---|---|---|---|---|---|---|---|---|---|
| 45468 | 5468 | 12/38 Crw | 65B | 05/64 | 45484 | 5484 | 10/43 Der | 66B | 02/64 |
| 45469 | 5469 | 12/38 Crw | 64A | 11/66 | 45485 | 5485 | 10/43 Der | 68C | 10/63 |
| 45470 | 5470 | 12/38 Crw | 68C | 09/64 | 45486 | 5486 | 10/43 Der | 67C | 12/65 |
| 45471 | 5471 | 12/38 Crw | 68B | 07/65 | 45487 | 5487 | 11/43 Der | 65F | 02/64 |
| 45472 | 5472 | 04/43 Der | 63A | 09/66 | 45488 | 5488 | 11/43 Der | 67A | 11/66 |
| 45473 | 5473 | 05/43 Der | 62B | 11/66 | 45489 | 5489 | 11/43 Der | 67B | 11/66 |
| 45474 | 5474 | 05/43 Der | 67C | 09/66 | 45490 | 5490 | 12/43 Der | 66B | 12/66 |
| 45475 | 5475 | 06/43 Der | 63A | 09/66 | 45491 | 5491 P | 12/43 Der | 68A | 07/65 |
| 45476 | 5476 | 07/43 Der | 63A | 10/64 | 45492 | 5492 | 01/44 Der | 66B | 12/66 |
| 45477 | 5477 | 07/43 Der | 64A | 08/66 | 45493 | 5493 | 01/44 Der | 68A | 01/68 |
| 45478 | 5478 | 08/43 Der | 64D | 12/66 | 45494 | 5494 | 01/44 Der | 5B | 09/67 |
| 45479 | 5479 | 08/43 Der | 67D | 05/64 | 45495 | 5495 | 02/44 Der | 11A | 03/67 |
| 45480 | 5480 | 08/43 Der | 68B | 08/66 | 45496 | 5496 | 02/44 Der | 66B | 06/64 |
| 45481 | 5481 | 09/43 Der | 68A | 09/67 | 45497 | 5497 | 04/44 Der | 67C | 02/64 |
| 45482 | 5482 | 09/43 Der | 65F | 06/64 | 45498 | 5498 | 04/44 Der | 66B | 06/65 |
| 45483 | 5483 | 09/43 Der | 64A | 12/66 | 45499 | 5499 | 04/44 Der | 65B | 07/65 |

*AW – Armstrong Whitworth, Crw – Crewe, Der – Derby, Hor – Horwich, VF – Vulcan Foundry*

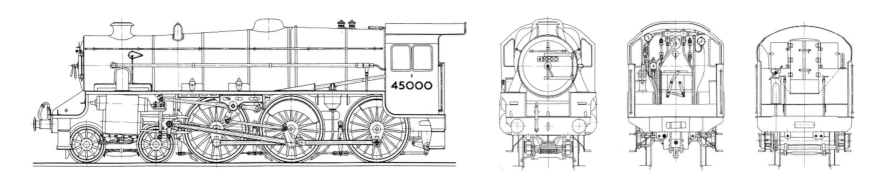

## ACKNOWLEDGEMENTS

This is a Perceptive Images 2018 © publication exclusively for Pen & Sword Books Ltd. Additional editorial information and specific images were supplied by my good friends David Anderson and John Chalcraft, whose encouragement and shared railway knowledge was invaluable.

Photographic libraries whose images have been included are Rail Photoprints Collection – http://railphotoprints.uk and the Mike Morant Collection – https://mikemorant.smugmug.com.

Additionally, thanks are due to a great many individuals who have allowed their valuable images to be included, and the appropriate credits are shown.

Further research about the class can be undertaken by consulting these websites and titles, and indeed others:

*Rail Info UK* www.railuk.info/steam/
*BR Database* www.brdatabase.info/
*Six Bells Junction* www.sixbellsjunction.co.uk

*British Railways Steam Locomotives 1948–1968* – Hugh Longworth Ian Allan Publishing 2005.
*The Stanier 4-6-0s of the LMS* – JWP Rowledge and Brian Reed David & Charles (Publishers) Ltd 1977
*Classic British Steam Locomotives* – Peter Herring Abbeydale Press 2000
*British Locomotive Classes* – *Ian Allan 1945*